SMALL ARMS

PISTOLS AND RIFLES

GREENHILL MILITARY MANUALS

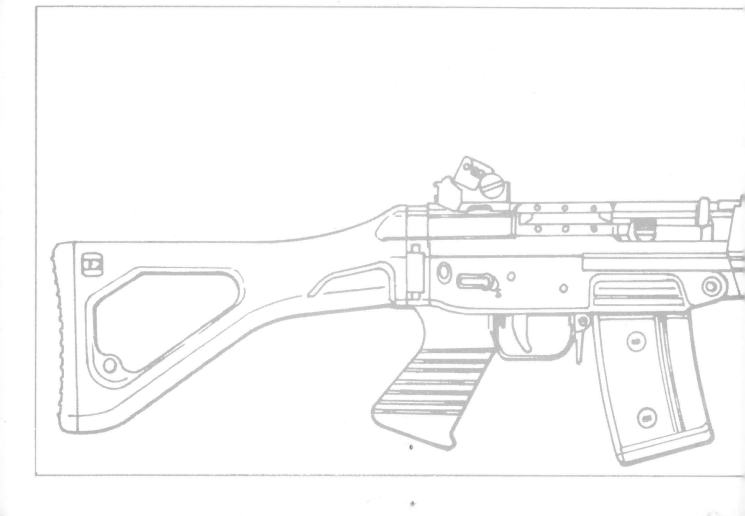

SMALL ARMS
PISTOLS & RIFLES

IAN V. HOGG
REVISED BY JOHN WALTER
ILLUSTRATED BY RAY HUTCHINS

GREENHILL MILITARY MANUALS

Greenhill Books, London
Stackpole Books, Pennsylvania

This edition of
Small Arms: Pistols and Rifles
first published 2003 by Greenhill Books, Lionel Leventhal Limited,
Park House, 1 Russell Gardens, London NW11 9NN
and
Stackpole Books, 5067 Ritter Road, Mechanicsburg, PA 17055, USA

British Library Cataloguing in Publication Data
Hogg, Ian V.
Small arms – New ed. – Greenhill military manuals
1. Pistols 2. Rifles 3. Pistols – design 4. Rifles - design
I. Title II. Hutchins, Ray III. Walter, John, 1951–
623.4'4

ISBN 1-85367-563-6

Library of Congress Cataloging-in-Publication Data
available

Printed and bound in Singapore by Kyodo Printing Company

Introduction

The firearms industry celebrated a few anniversaries at the start of the twenty-first century: of the Browning 'Old Model', the first really successful and widely sold automatic pistol on the commercial market; of the first Luger design; of Bergmann's first attempt to sell the idea of a 10mm cartridge; of the first Webley-Fosbery automatic revolver; and of the Benet-Mercie Hotchkiss machine gun ... not, perhaps, earth-shaking but all of some significance and illustrating the diversity of ideas flying about at the start of the previous century.

The subsequent 100 years saw a constant procession of innovative ideas and new designs. It would be rash to claim that firearms have reached the zenith of their development, but I think it true to say that they have now reached a level of technical excellence from which it will be extremely difficult, and prohibitively expensive in relation to any advantages gained, to move on. Recently the United States Army expended several hundred million dollars in a competition to find an Advanced Combat Rifle. After some years of work, four competing designs were exhaustively tested, and the results, carefully analysed, showed that the degree of improvement over the current service rifle was simply not worth the cost of replacement.

Similarly, it is probable that innovation is becoming rare because the expense is beyond the pocket of private companies. The days when a lone inventor laboured over his brain-child in a humble workshop, and then took it to a manufacturing company to be turned into a profitable venture, are almost over. Today it requires vast expenditure in research and development to bring a weapon to the point of production, and few companies now have such financial resources. The future of firearms development lies in international co-operation or state subsidies, or both.

Firearms design also seems to have reached a plateau. One hundred years ago new designs appeared every week, largely because inventors were trying to evade patents and find some original and novel way to make a gun work. Today, with every important feature out of patent protection, there is less incentive to be original: the worthwhile methods of construction and operation have survived, and are widely used; the worthless designs, innovation for the sake of being different, have all gone into oblivion. Certain features recur, and some mechanical ideas have been so widely accepted that almost every current designer applies them without stopping to think whether the solution might be reached by other means. One has only to consider the number of modern automatic pistols locking the breech into the ejection opening, or the number of gas-operated rifles using rotating bolts in a carrier, to recognise this commonality. Only one of the modern weapons shown here (the FN Five-seveN pistol) has an entirely new method of operation. Yet if you examine the patent records of the late nineteenth century you will find most of today's mechanisms and ideas illustrated and explained. The reason it has taken so long to put them into practice is simply that the technology of the nineteenth century lagged some way behind the ingenuity of the inventors. All of which is an introduction to the rest of this book, which is a representative showcase of modern, and some not so modern, pistols and rifles. Here are one or two elderly designs, to remind us of what went before, and a greater number of modern designs to indicate where we stand at the start of the new century.

The Future

1. Some designs will go on forever. This is the Browning BDA9 double-action automatic pistol, and as the component parts show, the mechanism is very little different to the first Colt automatic pistol developed by John Moses Browning in 1900. Browning improved his design after the First World War, and after being delayed by the economic slump in the early 1930s, it appeared as the Browning High-Power in 1935. This lasted unchanged for over fifty years, after which a double-action trigger mechanism changed it into the BDA9. There is no reason why this pistol should not make another fifty years of service; why change something when it is perfectly good?

2. Some designs defy all the odds and survive long past their sell-by date. This Afghan guerrilla is examining a Soviet Stechkin full-automatic pistol taken from a downed Soviet pilot. The Stechkin was virtually a mini-submachine gun, and almost uncontrollable. It did not last long in Soviet service, but was later disposed of to various places and will doubtless appear for several years yet in sundry trouble spots.

4. The rifle firing caseless ammunition has been tempting designers since the 1940s. The principal advantage is the saving in brass and hence weight: the soldier can carry three times as much ammunition as for a conventional rifle. The technical problems were immense, but were successfully solved in the late 1970s. The next ten years were taken up with perfecting the principles into a design that could be economically manufactured. This done, the design was ready for adoption when the entire world strategic picture changed overnight, the threat of Soviet aggression appeared to vanish and governments dramatically cut the amount of money they were prepared to spend on defence. The first victim was the caseless cartridge rifle. We shall see whether it re-appears in this century, or not.

3. The assault rifle has become the universal infantry arm, superseding the full-sized rifle firing a long-range cartridge. In conjunction, as here, with a sight capable of seeing in starlight, it becomes a formidable weapon which gives the soldier command of the battlefield throughout the entire 24 hours. The only problem technology has yet to solve is how to keep him awake for 24 hours every day.

CONTENTS

Rifles

GLOCK Model 17 Austria

Manufacturer: Glock GmbH,
Deutsche Wagram
(Variant Models: Models 17L, 18,
19, 20, 21, 22 and 23)

In the early 1980s the Austrian Army selected the **Glock 17** as their new service pistol. The Glock company were known for their manufacture of bayonets, knives and edged tools, but they had never ventured into the firearms business before, and their appearance with this novel and practical weapon was something of a shock. After the Austrian Army, the pistol was adopted by India, Jordan, Norway, The Philippines, Thailand and several other military and police forces around the world.

The Glock 17 is a recoil-operated pistol, using the familiar Browning system of dropping barrel controlled by a cam surface, and using the squared-off area of the breech to lock directly into the ejection port. No hammer is used; instead there is a self-cocking striker system. The first 5mm of trigger movement cocks the striker and releases an automatic firing-pin safety lock. Further pressure on the trigger then releases the striker to fire the

cartridge. There is no manual safety catch, but there is a small safety spur on the trigger.

Much of the Glock pistol is made from synthetic material, with the metal components moulded in; this gave rise to scare stories in the popular press, suggesting that the weapon would be a gift to terrorists since it would be invisible to airport X-Ray search. In fact some 60% of the weapon is of steel, and any X-Ray device will detect it instantly.

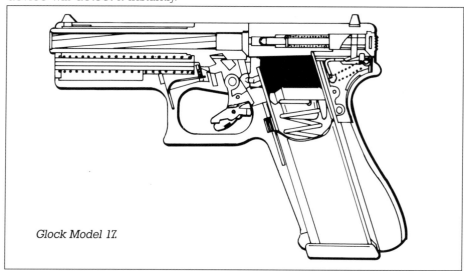

Glock Model 17.

10

Many variations of the Glock have been made since 1983, which is a tribute to the soundness of the basic design; indeed, the two millionth pistol was made in 1999.

The **Model 17L** has a 150mm barrel, intended for practical-pistol competitions and target shooting rather than service use; the **Model 19** is a 'compact' derivative, with an overall length of 177mm instead of the 188mm of the Model 17.

The **Models 20** (10mm) and **21** (.45 ACP) were introduced in 1990–91 to cater for purchasers who required more powerful chamberings. Both are slightly longer than the Model 17. The **Model 22** is little more than a Model 17 chambering the .40 Smith & Wesson cartridge, and the **Model 23** is the .40-calibre compact. The **Model 29** (10mm Auto) and **Model 30** (.45 ACP), each 170mm long, are also compact designs. Among the 'sub-compact' Glocks are the **Models 26** (9mm Parabellum) and **27** (.40 S&W), introduced in 1996.

The **Models 31, 32** and **33** are facsimiles of the Models 17, 19 and 26, but chamber the new .357 Auto cartridge; the **Models 34** (9mm Parabellum) and **35** (.40 S&W) are long-barrel guns with 10-round single-row magazines conforming with the US Gun Control Act of 1994.

The **Model 18**, the one major departure from the basic design, has an additional fire selector mechanism and an enlarged magazine, turning the Model 17 into a machine pistol capable of automatic fire. The principal components of the Models 17 and 18 are not interchangeable, preventing unauthorised conversions, even though the basic mechanism remains the same.

Specification (Model 17):

Calibre: 9mm Parabellum
Operation: Short recoil, semi-automatic
Length overall: 188mm
Weight, empty: 650g
Barrel: 114mm, 6 grooves, right-hand twist
Magazine: 17-round box
Muzzle velocity: 350 m/sec

Above: Glock Model 17L with 153mm barrel.

Above: Machine pistol Model 18 with the optional 33-round extended magazine.

Left: The 10mm calibre Model 20.

11

STEYR M-SERIES

Manufacturer: Steyr-Mannlicher GmbH, Steyr
(Models: M-40, M-9)

As can be seen from the **Steyr AUG** and **Advanced Combat Rifle**, in later entries in the book, Steyr-Mannlicher are no strangers to the use of high-strength plastic materials in the construction of firearms. An eight-ton truck can drive over an AUG rifle without doing it any serious harm or impairing either its reliability or its accuracy. Steyr-Mannlicher have now extended that expertise to pistols with their **M-Series**, announced in 1999.

Comparisons with the **Glock** are inevitable, but apart from their use of plastic and their common adoption of the Colt/Browning dropping barrel method of locking the breech, there is little similarity, and Steyr have produced some interesting features which indicate original lines of thought.

One of the most obvious of these is the 'Triangle-Trapezoid' sighting system. The foresight, viewed from the rear, is a very distinct white triangle. The rear sight has a wide notch like the lower part of a triangle, with sides sloping parallel to the sides of the foresight. To take aim the foresight is positioned inside this notch so that it is central, with its tip level with the top of the notch and the sides equidistant from each side of the notch. In effect it is rather like an aperture back sight, in that the firer instinctively positions the foresight in the centre of the

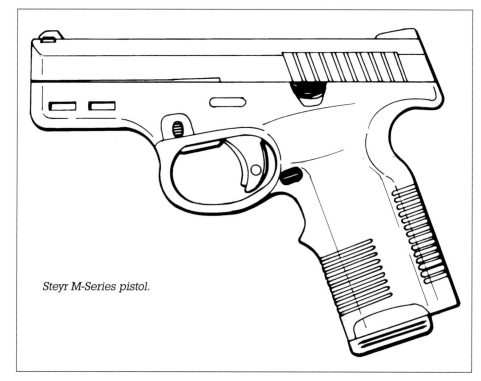

Steyr M-Series pistol.

'aperture' without giving it much thought. The edges of the notch are also white, so that the sight is well adapted to firing in poor light conditions.

Safety is the other major concern, with an automatic trigger safety, a manually applied safety which can be very quickly released by a movement of the trigger finger, and a key-locking safety which not only prevents the pistol being fired but also prevents it being dismantled. Other features include a loaded chamber indicator which protrudes from the rear of the slide and which can be both seen and felt, and an ambidextrous magazine release button. The firing mechanism is, of course, a hammerless system giving a very short single-action pull; a double-action-only version is available as an option.

The M-Series pistol is available in two forms, the M-40 and the M-9, the difference being in the calibres of .40 Smith & Wesson or 9mm Parabellum.

Specification:
Calibre: 9mm Parabellum or .40 Smith & Wesson
Operation: Recoil, striker fired
Length overall: 180mm
Weight, empty: 780g
Barrel: 100mm
Magazine: 14 (9mm) or 12 (.40) rounds
Muzzle velocity: 350 m/sec (9mm); 285 m/sec (.40)

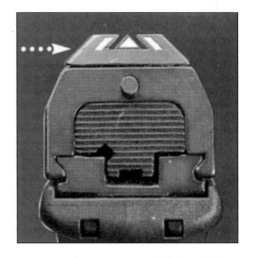

Above right: A rear view of the Triangle-Trapezoid sights, showing how they fall into alignment almost instinctively as they are brought up to the aim.

Right: A loaded-chamber indicator at the rear of the slide gives visual and tactile confirmation of a cartridge in the chamber.

13

FN-BROWNING GP-35 (High Power)   Belgium

Manufacturer: FN Herstal SA, Herstal
(Variant Models: GP-35, Mark 2, Mark 3, Mark 3S, BDA-9)

One of the oldest military-pistol designs to survive in regular service into the 21st century, this was based on a refinement of the US Army M1911 Colt-Browning *(q.v.)* begun by John Browning shortly before the First World War began in 1914.

Major changes were made to the trigger linkage, and a solid block of metal with a curved slotted path, engaging with a slide-stop pin, was used to unlock the barrel instead of a swinging link.

It is assumed that Browning intended to offer the pistol to Fabrique Nationale d'Armes de Guerre, but that the German invasion of Belgium put paid to work until the early 1920s. Many 9mm-calibre prototypes were made, and the first patents were sought in Europe and the USA in 1923. Unfortunately, Browning died unexpectedly in 1926.

Work was continued by the Fabrique Nationale design bureau, under the leadership of Dieudonné Saive. A comparison of the pre- and post-1926 prototypes shows many changes – in particular, the substitution of an external hammer for the original striker, and the adoption of a staggered-row magazine that could hold thirteen rounds.

Work had been completed by 1928, but the Great Depression of 1929–35 forced FN to shelve production plans until 1935. The gun was then adopted by the Belgian Army as the **GP-35**, and export orders were obtained from Lithuania, Latvia and China. However, only about 35,000 pistols had been completed by 1940, when the Germans once again seized the factory, and very few deliveries had been made outside Belgium.

The Fabrique Nationale factory in Herstal continued to make GP-35 pistols under German supervision, the resulting **Pistole 640 (b)** being issued to the Wehrmacht in large quantities. Guns of this type can usually be identified by German military inspectors' markings, notably on the slide and frame.

Shortly before the Germans seized Herstal, key technicians escaped first to France and then to Britain, taking

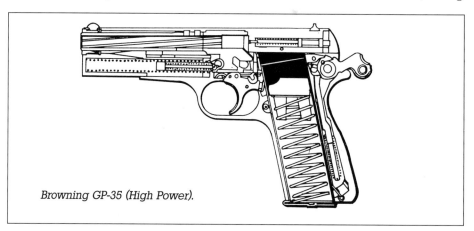

Browning GP-35 (High Power).

with them drawings of the pistol. Though no progress could be made in Britain, for fear of jeopardising the supply of existing weapons, a decision was taken to begin production in Canada. The work was entrusted to the John Inglis Company of Toronto, which was also making Bren Guns, with the primary intention of supplying the Chinese Nationalist forces. However, Canadian-made pistols were also supplied to the Canadian and British Armies. Work resumed in Herstal after the end of the Second World War.

Often known simply as the **High-Power** or 'Hi-Power' (a translation of Grande Puissance), the pistol has been exceptionally successful. It has been adopted by military, paramilitary and police units in nearly seventy countries; made under licence in Indonesia; and copied by the Cao Dai in Cambodia. The British Army adopted it officially in 1954.

Introduced in the 1970s, the **Mark 2** had 'anatomical' grips, an ambidextrous safety catch, wider sights and an oxidised finish.

Production ceased in the early 1980s. The **Mark 3** of 1988 was practically the same as the Mk 2, but had a strengthened slide, changes in the dimensions of some individual components to improve reliability, and exchangeable target/combat sights. The **Mark 3S**, intended specifically for police service, had an additional automatic firing-pin safety system.

Realising that the GP-35 was approaching obsolescence, FN developed the **BDA-9**. Introduced in 1983, this was essentially an

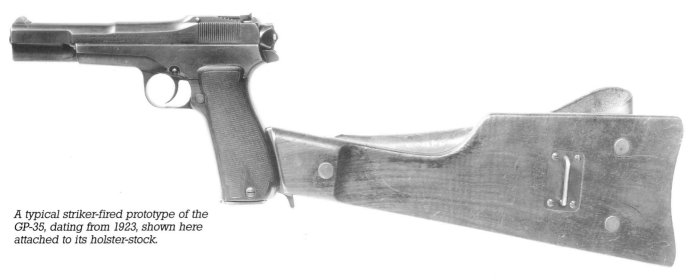

A typical striker-fired prototype of the GP-35, dating from 1923, shown here attached to its holster-stock.

enhanced GP-35, retaining the locking system, but with a new double-action trigger mechanism; a de-cocking lever that was duplicated on both sides of the frame; an automatic firing-pin safety system similar to that of the Mark 3S; and a new fourteen-round magazine. The magazine-release catch was customarily fitted for right-handed use, but could easily be reversed to suit left-handers.

The BDA-9 is loaded in the usual manner by pulling back the slide and releasing it. This leaves the hammer cocked. Pulling the trigger fires the gun; alternatively, the de-cocking lever can be pressed upward to release the hammer, which, slowed by a brake, falls at moderate speed until it is stopped by the de-cocking safety notch before it can strike the firing pin.

Releasing pressure on the de-cocking lever allows it to spring back, and the gun can be carried in safety. Pulling through on the trigger is enough to fire. The final movement of the trigger, which releases the hammer, also raises the automatic safety block from engagement with the firing pin so that the falling hammer hits the pin, drives it forward and fires the cartridge. The firing pin is automatically locked in a safe position at all other times, preventing the hammer reaching the striker should the de-cocking safety fail.

The shape of the BDA is unmistakably Browning, excepting the trigger guard, which is elongated – a double-action trigger has a longer pull than a single-action type – and shaped at the front to accommodate a two-handed grip. The grips are shaped to give an anatomically-correct surface, and the back sight can be adjusted laterally by an armourer.

The standard gun was accompanied by a 'compact' **BDA-9M** ('Medium'), and a 'sub-compact' **BDA-9C** ('Compact') with a greatly abbreviated grip that

A pre-war example of the FN-Browning GP-35.

required a special magazine holding just eight rounds.

Specification (GP-35):
Calibre: 9mm Parabellum
Operation: Short recoil, semi-automatic
Length overall: 197mm
Weight, empty: 990g
Barrel: 118mm, 6 grooves, right-hand twist, one turn in 250mm
Magazine: 13-round box
Muzzle velocity: 335 m/sec

Right & below: The FN BDA-9 is the double-action version of the older High Power GP-35. The resemblance between this and the older pistol is easily seen, though there are small differences in the trigger guard and an ambidextrous decocking lever has been added.

Manufacturer: FN Herstal SA, Herstal

This is a self-cocking semi-automatic firing the same cartridge as the P-90 personal defence weapon. The trigger action is rather unusual in that pressure on the trigger first compresses the firing pin spring and then releases the firing pin. Unless the trigger is pressed, the firing pin is never under any sort of pressure, and thus there is no manual safety catch.

Surprisingly, for a weapon of such power, the **Five-seveN** operates on the delayed blowback principle. The slide carries two notches on its under-surface. Set into the frame is a cross-shaft carrying two connected lugs. The barrel is a loose fit in the slide, and when the barrel and slide are assembled to the frame, a slotted lug beneath the chamber is so placed that the slot lines up with the cross-shaft. On firing, the pressure in the chamber forces the bullet up the barrel, and the friction and torque of the bullet's movement tends to thrust the barrel forward. At the same time the gas pressure forces the cartridge case back and puts

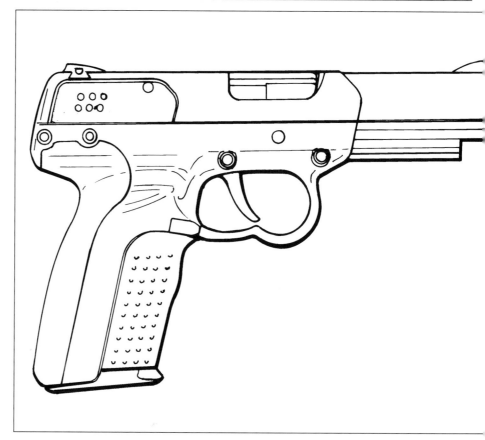

FN Five-seveN pistol.

pressure on the slide to move to the rear. Barrel and slide move rearward together about 3mm, at which point the slide notches engage the upstanding lugs on the cross shaft and the slide is halted. As the bullet leaves the barrel, so the friction and torque cease and the barrel is free to move backwards. This causes the slotted lug to move over the cross shaft and rotate it so that the twin lugs disengage from the notches in the slide, allowing the slide to continue moving rearwards to perform the usual extraction and reloading cycle while the barrel remains stationary. It all sounds very complicated but works with perfect efficiency.

The cartridge is considerably longer than the average pistol round, but the grip nevertheless fits the hand well and the recoil impulse is somewhat less than a 9mm Parabellum cartridge, so that the weapon is easily controlled. Introduced in 1995, it is still being evaluated by several armies and it remains to be seen whether it will replace the **High-Power** as the major FN pistol of the 21st century.

Specification:
Calibre: 5.7mm
Operation: Recoil, rotating barrel
Length overall: 208mm
Weight, empty: 618g
Barrel: 122.5mm, 6 grooves, right-hand twist
Magazine: 20-round detachable box
Muzzle velocity: approx. 650 m/sec

Above: In spite of the cartridge's length and power, the Five-seveN fits the hand well and the recoil is not excessive.

Below: Although a delayed blowback system is intricate, field-stripping is quite a simple process.

Manufacturer: State arsenals
(Variant Model: Type 67)

The **Type 64** is unusual in being built only with an integral silencer; there is no unsilenced version.

The frame is extended forward to carry the silencing system, which is a bulbous cylinder which contains a central wire mesh tube holding a number of rubber discs and which is surrounded by perforated metal sleeves. The fixed barrel is quite short, and after the bullet leaves the muzzle it passes into the wire mesh tube and through the series of rubber discs before leaving the end of the silencer. The gas which follows the bullet is forced to swirl around the perforated sleeves and is stopped from following the bullet by the self-sealing action of the rubber discs. This swirling gradually reduces the gas velocity and heat so that when the gas finally finds its way out at the front of the silencer it is moving comparatively slowly and generates almost no noise at all.

The rear of the frame carries a conventional type of slide which is driven back by the gas pressure in the fired case in the normal blowback manner. The slide contains a striker, which is cocked on the return stroke and held by a sear connected to the trigger. The slide is unusual in having a rotating-lug bolt head as its front end. There is a manual catch which can be set, after the breech has been closed, to lock the bolt to the barrel by means of the rotating head. Once this has been done, the blowback action is prevented and the breech remains closed after firing. The weapon is taken from the scene and at some location where noise is no longer important the slide is then unlocked and manually operated to eject the empty case and reload.

The cartridge used with this pistol is known as the 'Type 64' and is also unique; although it resembles the common ·32 ACP it is, in fact, rimless rather than semi-rimmed and the powder charge is specially selected to assist in the silencing.

The **Type 67** is an improved model; the principle of operation is the same but the silencer unit is a plain cylinder, making the weapon less bulky and easier to carry in a holster.

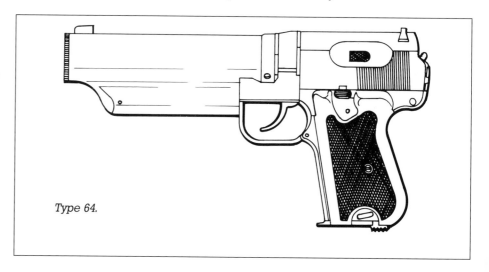

Type 64.

Specification:

Calibre: 7.65mm Type 64
Operation: Blowback, with locked breech option
Length overall: 222mm
Weight, empty: 1.81kg
Barrel: 95mm
Magazine: 9-round box
Muzzle velocity: 205 m/sec

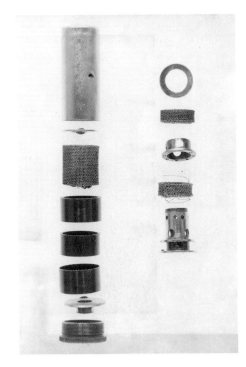

Above: The Type 67 pistol is an improved Type 64, the silencer being a neater and more efficient design. It is purely for use by clandestine units, to remove sentries and guard dogs without alerting the neighbourhood.

Left: The component parts of the Type 67 silencer, showing the gauze cylinders packed with absorbent material. The Type 64 layout is similar though of different shape.

Right: The Type 64 silenced pistol is easily recognised by the shape of the chamber beneath the barrel.

ČZ75 Series   Czechoslovakia/Czech Republic

Manufacturer: Česka Zbrojovka, Uhersky Brod
(Variant Model: ČZ85)

This was never a Czech service pistol because, like all Warsaw Pact countries, the Czechs did not use the 9mm Parabellum cartridge in military service. It was originally produced for export, and has been very successful in that respect, gaining a very high reputation for reliability and accuracy; it was later adopted by various elements of the Czech police force. The basic design has been copied by several other makers in various countries for commercial sale.

The ČZ75 is recoil-operated, using the well-tried Browning dropping barrel system, controlled by a shaped cam beneath the breech end. Slide and frame are precision castings carefully machined and well finished, and the grips are either of plastic or walnut. The trigger mechanism is double-action, and the slide-mounted safety catch disconnects the trigger from the hammer; it does not lower the hammer. It is of interest that the original design used a half-cock

notch on the hammer; this was then removed at the insistence of production engineers to make manufacture simpler, but after two or three accidents reported from West Germany the half-cock notch was reinstated.

All the operating controls – safety catch, slide stop lever and magazine catch – are on the left side of the frame to suit right-handed firers. After several competing designers developed weapons with controls suited for right or left-handed use,

the ČZ85 pistol was developed. This is basically the same pistol but with the manual safety catch and slide stop lever duplicated on the right side of the weapon to make it convenient for left-handed use. The top of the slide is ribbed, to reduce light reflection, and some small internal changes have been made to simplify manufacture and also to improve the smooth action of the firing mechanism. The rear sight has been made laterally adjustable by means of a screw so that firers can

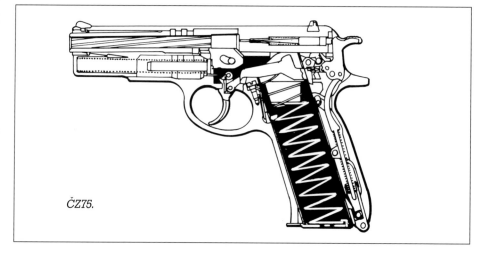

ČZ75.

make adjustments without requiring the services of a gunsmith. Both models are currently in production.

Changes made since the introduction of the ČZ85 have included the upgrading of the original gun to '75B' or '85B' standards in 1986, and the advent of compact and de-cocking versions of the ČZ75. Target-shooting versions have also been offered as **ČZ75 IPSC**. The **ČZ85B Combat** (1999) has changes to the sights, trigger and magazine, and lacks the firing-pin safety. .22 rimfire training/sport pistols, known as the **ČZ75 Kadet** and **ČZ85 Kadet**, were also introduced in the late 1990s.

Operating the safety catch on the ČZ85, an improved version of the original ČZ75.

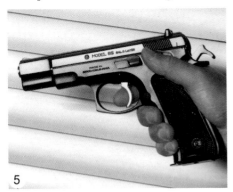

The ČZ75 was developed entirely for export, being a non-standard Warsaw pact calibre. It has been widely sold abroad, and the simplicity of its construction has attracted a number of licensees and copyists in Britain, the USA, Italy and other countries.

The ČZ75 proved to be exceptionally popular, though initially difficult to acquire in the West. This changed with the collapse of Communism and a new private-enterprise spirit that pervaded countries such as Czechoslovakia, Hungary and Yugoslavia.

In addition, the ČZ75 has been licensed to various manufacturers, for example Tanfoglio in Italy and ITM (*see 'Sphinx'*) in Switzerland. Guns may be found with the marks of Springfield Armory, Inc., and the IMI

Jericho 941 pistol (*q.v.*), now often marketed as the 'Baby Eagle', is also a straightforward derivative of the basic design with fashionably squared contours (particularly the trigger guard) that hide its origins. Consequently, ČZ-type pistols will be found with a bewildering variety of features and equally diverse markings. Tanfoglio guns, in particular, may chamber .41 AE or 9x21mm cartridges or show adaptations for practical-pistol target shooting.

The Czech manufacturer, meanwhile, has developed the **ČZ100**. This has a SIG-type locking action, camming the top surface of the chamber-block portion of the barrel into the ejection opening in the slide. Extensive use is made of synthetic parts, but it is still too early to gauge whether the new design will be able to supersede the ČZ75/ČZ85 series successfully.

Specification (ČZ75):
Calibre: 9mm Parabellum
Operation: Short recoil, semi-automatic
Length overall: 203mm
Weight, empty: 980g
Barrel: 120mm, 6 grooves, right-hand twist, one turn in 250mm
Magazine: 15-round box
Muzzle velocity: 338 m/sec

A typical Tanfoglio TA-21, in 9x21mm chambering.

The new ČZ100, which introduces SIG-inspired features to Czech handgun design.

HECKLER & KOCH USP   Germany

Manufacturer: Heckler & Koch GmbH, Oberndorf/Neckar

The **USP** (Universal Self-loading Pistol) was designed with the intention of incorporating all the various features which military and law enforcement agencies appeared to find vital. It appeared in 1994 and introduced the first locked breech pistol from Heckler & Koch. The pistol is recoil-operated, using a form of Browning dropping barrel lock; instead of the usual hinged link or cam, there is a shaped claw beneath the breech which, as the slide and barrel move rearward, hooks into a cam surface to withdraw the barrel from engagement with the slide. Locking is performed by the currently popular method of forming the chamber area of the barrel into a rectangular lump and forcing this into a rectangular ejection opening in the slide.

The design also incorporates a patented recoil damping system. The return spring rod carries two springs, a buffer spring and the normal return spring. On firing, as the barrel moves back it pulls on the guide rod and compresses the short buffer spring, absorbing some of the recoil. As the barrel disconnects from the slide and the slide is free to move independently, it then places the return spring under compression in the usual way, and at the same time the buffer spring is relieved of the pull and re-asserts itself, moving forward. As the slide comes to the end of the recoil stroke, so it also begins to compress the buffer spring once more, giving an additional brake to the recoil movement and stopping it. Both the springs then re-assert themselves and the slide goes forward, loading the fresh round and returning the barrel to battery.

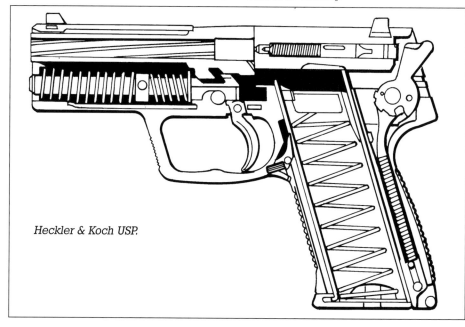

Heckler & Koch USP.

The slide and barrel are of steel, as might be expected, but the frame is of polymer plastic, exceptionally tough and dimensionally stable. The sights are provided with white luminous dots for aiming in poor light, and all the controls are ambidextrous so that the pistol can be used equally well in either hand.

The **USP** is made in no fewer than nine variant versions, largely because the trigger and firing mechanisms are modular and can be readily changed. Thus the action can be double action or self-cocking only, and the safety systems can be varied, leading to the following options:

1. Double action with manual safety/de-cocking lever on left side of frame.

2. Double action with manual safety/de-cocking lever on right side of frame.

3. Double action, no safety, de-cocking lever on left side of frame.

4. Double action, no safety, de-cocking lever on right side of frame.

5. Self-cocking only, with manual safety catch on left side of frame.

6. Self-cocking only, with manual safety catch on right side of frame.

7. Self-cocking only, no safety catch, no de-cocking lever.

8. Double action, manual safety catch on left side of frame.

9. Double action, manual safety catch on right side of frame.

Specification:
Calibre: 9mm Parabellum or .40 Smith & Wesson or .45 ACP
Operation: Recoil, double action, hammer fired
Length overall: 194mm (9mm and .40); 200mm (.45)
Weight, empty: 770g (9mm); 830g (.40); 887g (.45)
Barrel: 108mm (9mm and .40); 112mm (.45); polygonal
Magazine: 15 (9mm) or 13 (.40) or 12 (.45) rounds
Muzzle velocity: 350 m/sec (9mm); 285 m/sec (.40); 270 m/sec (.45)

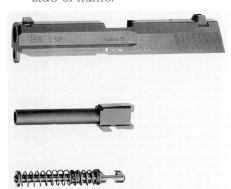

Left: The slide, barrel and return spring assembly stripped. Note the dual spring system which gives additional buffering to the recoil of the slide.

Right: The frame and magazine are of fibre-reinforced polymer plastic, with stainless steel inserts in those areas subjected to the greatest stress during operation.

HECKLER & KOCH P7 — Germany

Manufacturer: Heckler & Koch GmbH, Oberndorf/Neckar
(Variant Models: P7M8, P7M13, P7M45, P7K3, P7PT)

In the middle 1970s the German Federal Police Office issued a specification demanding a pistol of about 9mm calibre, a minimum muzzle energy of 500 Joules, a minimum muzzle velocity of 350 metres per second, and a minimum magazine capacity of six shots. It was to weigh no more than 1kg, be no more than 180mm long and have a barrel of eight to ten calibres length. Most importantly the first shot had to be fired without the need to operate any form of safety catch or lock and the pistol had to be safe against any form of accidental discharge.

This was a stiff bill to meet, and only a handful of makers bothered to try it. Among them was Heckler & Koch with their **PSP** (Polizei Selbstlade Pistole), which was so successful that it was adopted by several German police and security forces as the **'Pistole 7'**, after which H&K renamed it the **P7**.

The basic **P7** has two unique features. Firstly it is a delayed blowback in which the delay is provided by a

piston, connected to the slide, acting inside a cylinder in the frame. Propellant gas passes into this cylinder on firing and resists the rearward movement of the piston due to the recoil of the slide. The second unusual feature is the 'squeeze-cocking' system employed; the front of the grip is a movable bar which is instinctively squeezed inwards when the butt is grasped. This squeezing movement cocks the firing pin, and pressure on

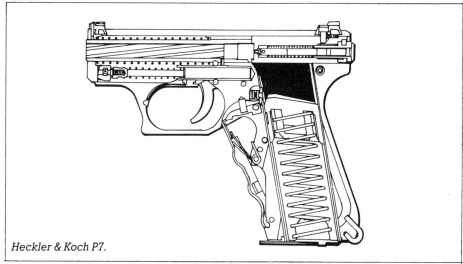

Heckler & Koch P7.

the trigger can then release it to fire the pistol. As soon as the grip is released, the firing pin is uncocked, so there is no need for a safety catch.

The **P7** is now available in a number of forms; the **P7M13** is the standard weapon; the **P7M8** has a more slender butt and an eight-round magazine. The **P7K3** is a simple blowback, but retains the squeeze-cocking feature and is available with interchangeable barrels and other parts, allowing the choice of ·22, 7·65mm ACP and 9mm Short calibres. The **P7PT** resembles the **P7M13** but is designed solely for use with plastic-bullet training ammunition.

The Heckler & Koch P7M10 showing the odd-shaped magazine which reduces a double column to a single feed for reliability. The drawing (left) shows the mechanism of the grip-cocking device, which ensures that should the weapon be dropped it will be in a safe condition before it reaches the ground.

Specification:
Calibre: 9mm Parabellum
Operation: Delayed blowback, semi-automatic
Length overall: 171mm
Weight, empty: 800g
Barrel: 105mm, polygonal, right-hand twist
Magazine: 13-round box
Muzzle velocity: 350 m/sec.

WALTHER PP & PPK   Germany

Manufacturer: Waffenfabrik Carl Walther, Zella-Mehlis; Carl Walther GmbH, Ulm/Donau, Germany
(Variants: PP, PPK, PPK/S, TPH)

Many 19th-century revolvers had successfully incorporated double-action trigger systems, allowing the gun to be fired simply by pulling through on the trigger lever to raise and then release the hammer. However, prior to 1914, only Alois Tomiška and Sergey Korovin had been able to adapt the principles to semi-automatic pistols. Hitherto it had been necessary to load the pistol and carry it cocked, relying on the safety catch, or carry it empty and cock it when the need arose. Neither scenario was suited to police and military service.

Tomiška pistols were made in Austria and Czechoslovakia as the 'Little Tom', though the chronology is still unclear. However, rights to the Tomiška patents were definitely purchased by Fritz Walther in the early 1920s and the **PP** or **Polizei-Pistole** appeared in 1929 – the first successful application of the double-action principles to a gun genuinely

suited to paramilitary and police service.

A simple blowback weapon of sound design and excellent manufacture, the Walther had a double-action system that allowed the pistol to be loaded, leaving the hammer cocked as usual. Applying the safety catch then retracted or locked the firing pin and then allowed the hammer to drop safely into the uncocked position. A firer

merely had to release the safety catch and pull the trigger to lift and drop the hammer and fire the pistol; after that, the action of the slide cocked the hammer and subsequent shots were fired in the usual single-action mode.

For those who required greater precision in the first shot, and who had the time, it was easy to thumb-cock the hammer and fire the first shot in single-action mode; this

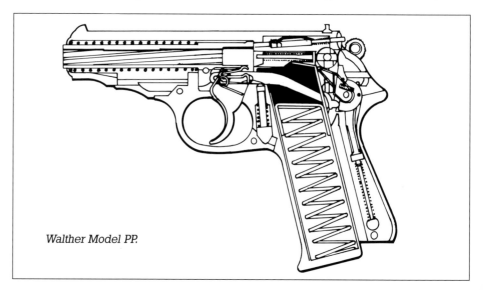

Walther Model PP.

30

demands less effort on the trigger and delivers better accuracy.

The PP was developed to provide uniformed police officers with a holster weapon, though it was also very successful commercially. The first guns were chambered for the 7.65mm Auto Pistol cartridge, but .22 rimfire, 6.35mm Auto and 9mm Short options were subsequently added (though only small quantities were offered in .22 rimfire and 6.35mm calibre).

The PP also embodies a loaded-chamber indicator in the form of a small pin that protrudes from the rear of the slide when a cartridge is loaded, a signal that can be seen or felt in the dark.

The instantaneous success of the PP in police service promoted the development of a smaller version that could be more readily concealed about the person of plain-clothes officers. The **PPK** – a pistol for the 'Kripo' or *Kriminalpolizei*, the detective branch of the German police forces – appeared in late 1931. It was little more than a smaller PP, reduced in length and height, with appropriately reduced magazine capacity.

The double-action trigger mechanism and safety arrange-ments remained the same, but the design of the frame was changed. The butt of the PP was a machined forging with an integral back strap and separate grip-plates. The PPK butt, however, was a simple open-box framework that relied on an all-enveloping plastic moulding to fit the hand. In addition, since the butt was rather short, the magazine base had a small plastic finger rest.

Many thousands of PPs and PPKs had been made by 1939, often for service with the police or paramilitary organisations such as the Nazi Party's *Sturm Abteilung* (SA).

A photograph of an Ulm-marked PPK/S.

When the Second World War began, supplies were redirected to the armed forces. These can usually be identified by military inspectors' marks, notably on the slide and frame. The PP was customarily issued to non-combatants, freeing P. 08 (Luger) and P. 38 (Walther) weapons for front-line service, but others were purchased by officers (particularly Luftwaffe personnel) who needed a compact self-defence weapon.

The quality of manufacture and finish declined towards the end of the war, and the markings were reduced to the Walther code ('ac'), the date and a serial number. Work stopped in April 1945, but Walther was subsequently able to licence production of the PP and PPK to Manurhin of Mulhouse in Alsace, German territory prior to 1945 and possibly more sympathetic to the project than other parts of France would have been.

The PP/PPK series has also been extensively copied, usually without benefit of licence or after the patents had expired. The Turkish Kirrikale (or 'MKE') and the Hungarian Walam or 48.M pistols are typical examples. The Russian Makarov (q.v.) is just one of many designs that drew its inspiration, if not detailed design, from the Polizei Pistole.

In the 1960s the PPK became very popular in the USA as an off-duty pistol for police officers, but the Gun Control Act of 1968 laid down a minimum depth of four inches for imported handguns; the PPK measured 3.9 inches from top of slide to bottom of the butt, cutting it out of a lucrative market.

The **PPK/S** was developed especially for sale in the USA, amalgamating the frame of the PP with the slide and barrel of the PPK; while the length remained the same as the latter, depth increased to 4.1 inches and thus the hybrid became legally acceptable. The **PP Super** was a short-lived 1970s' variant of the

The PP Super.

PP chambered for the 9mm Police cartridge; it could be distinguished by the shape of the trigger guard, which was much squarer than normal.

Introduced in Europe in 1968, the **TPH** is virtually a scaled-down PPK chambered for .22 rimfire or 6.35mm cartridges. Just 135mm long, the TPH makes an excellent vest-pocket pistol, though the low power of its ammunition precludes military or police applications.

Production of the PP/PPK series returned to Ulm/Donau in 1964, though the earliest Walther-marked guns were assembled from Manurhin-made parts. Interarms, Walther's US distributor, began production of the 'PP American' and 'PPK American' in a factory in Alexandria, Virginia, in the late 1970s. An American-made TPH followed, circumventing the provisions of the Gun Control Act. However, Interarms ceased work in 2000, and Walther has now also stopped making the PP/PPK series. There has even been an attempt to import a Walther clone, the Hungarian-made Walam, into the USA under the 'PPK/S' designation.

Specification (Walther PP):
Calibre: .22RF, 6.35mm, 7.65mm, 9mm Short
Operation: Blowback, semi-automatic
Length overall: 162mm
Weight, empty: 710g
Barrel: 85mm, 6 grooves, right-hand twist
Magazine: 8-round box
Muzzle velocity: 290 m/sec (7.65mm)

Specification (Walther PPK):
Calibre: .22RF, 6.35mm, 7.65mm, 9mm Short
Operation: Blowback, semi-automatic
Length: 148mm
Weight, empty: 590g
Barrel: 80mm, 6 grooves, right-hand twist
Magazine: 7-round box
Muzzle velocity: 275 m/sec (7.65mm)

The Hungarian FÉG 48.M or 'Walam' pistol was a close copy of the PP.

The Turkish Kirrikale, also known as the 'MKE', was another Walther clone, created soon after the end of the Second World War.

WALTHER P38 **Germany**

Manufacturer: Carl Walther GmbH and others

The German Army adopted the Parabellum (Luger) in 1908 and it served them very well; but in the mid 1930s they decided that a more modern design which would be easier and cheaper to manufacture should replace it, and called for suggestions. Walther replied by producing an enlarged version of the PP in 9mm Parabellum, but the Germany Army would not accept a blowback pistol in that calibre.

Walther's next attempt was a locked breech pistol using an internal hammer; this was refused on the grounds that invisible hammers could be cocked or uncocked and nobody could tell which. Finally Walther produced their 'Heeres Pistole' with locked breech and visible hammer, and this was accepted by the Army, who adopted it as their **'Pisole 38'** in 1938.

The **P38** had an exposed barrel which carried a locking wedge beneath it; when the pistol was ready to fire this wedge locked the barrel and slide together. On firing, barrel and slide recoiled a short distance, and then the wedge was cammed down to unlock it from the slide and halt the barrel. The slide continued rearwards to extract and eject the spent case and cock the hammer, then returned to chamber a new cartridge and, pushing the barrel forward, lifted the lug to re-lock the breech.

In addition, the double-action trigger and drop-hammer safety catch of the Models PP and PPK was carried over into the **P38**, making it the first military-calibre pistol to use the double-action

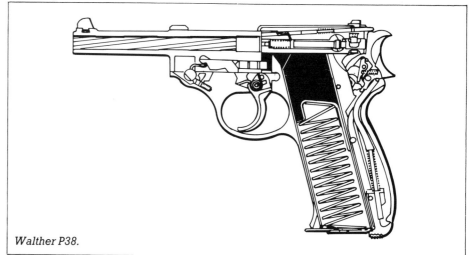

Walther P38.

trigger system. The 'loaded chamber indicator' was also adopted.

Although it proved to be very little cheaper than the Parabellum, the **P38** was certainly easier and quicker to manufacture, but wartime demands were too much for Walther and other companies also made the **P38**, while smaller firms made various components.

Walther resumed production of the **P38** in 1957 and it was re-adopted by the Bundeswehr as the **'Pistole 1'**. It has also been adopted by other military and police forces. A short-barrel version, the **P38K** was developed in the mid-1970s; this had the barrel cut down and the front sight mounted on the front end of the slide. Another shortened version was the **P4**, with a barrel length midway between the **P38** and **P38K**. Neither stayed in production for very long.

Specification:
Calibre: 9mm Parabellum
Operation: Short recoil, semi-automatic
Length overall: 213mm
Weight, empty: 960g
Barrel: 127mm, 6 grooves, right-hand twist
Magazine: 8-round box
Muzzle velocity: 350 m/sec.

The Walther P38K was a shortened version of the P38 intended as a heavy-calibre police weapon, but although a perfectly sound gun it did not meet the modern safety requirements demanded by the German police in the 1970s and was therefore replaced by the P5.

WALTHER P5   Germany

Manufacturer: Carl Walther GmbH,
Ulm/Donau, Germany
(Variant Models: P5 Compact;
P1A1)

Like many other European designs, the inspiration for the **P5** came from a demand by the German Federal Police Office for a new pistol in the middle 1970s. They demanded double-action triggers, large capacity magazines, and the minimum of preparation before opening fire, and this led to a complete new generation of weapons. The **P5** is an updated version of the P38 design. It uses the same method of breech locking, the same trigger mechanism and generally resembles the P38 except that instead of the familiar protruding barrel and open-topped slide it has a short barrel and an all-enveloping slide which is similar to most other automatic pistols.

The safety system, however, was drastically revised in order to meet the police requirements. The safety catch was moved to the left side of the frame and has become primarily a de-cocking lever with safety functions as a by-product. The safety of the weapon is provided by an automatic system built in to the firing pin area. The firing

pin is normally out of line, the rear end being pressed down by a spring so that the rear end of the firing pin lies opposite a recessed section of the pistol's hammer; thus, should the hammer fall for any reason the recessed part will enclose the firing pin end, and the bulk of the hammer will strike the body of the slide. When the trigger is pressed, a trip lever on the hammer mechanism is actuated, and this lifts the firing pin against the spring pressure and aligns it properly

with the striking face of the hammer. Continued pressure on the trigger releases the hammer to strike the pin, and as soon as the trigger is released the pin is forced back into the safe position.

The **P5** was adopted by a number of German police forces and also by the Netherlands police and Portuguese and other armies.

In 1988 the **P5 Compact** was introduced; this, as the name implies, is a shortened version of the **P5** with the

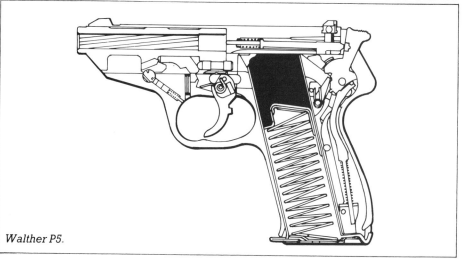

Walther P5.

same mechanical features. The **P1A1** followed this, and is virtually the **P5** but with the addition of a positive cross-bolt safety catch in the slide and with the magazine release placed on the heel of the butt instead of behind the trigger.

The **P5** is also produced in 7·65mm Parabellum and 9x21mm IMI chambering to special order.

The Walther P5 is based upon the same breech locking system as the P38 but incorporates a greatly revised and improved set of safety devices to ensure that the weapon can never be fired inadvertently.

Specification:
Calibre: 9mm Parabellum
Operation: Short recoil, semi-automatic
Length overall: 180mm
Weight, empty: 795g
Barrel: 90mm, 6 grooves, right-hand twist
Magazine: 8-round box
Muzzle velocity: 350 m/sec.

WALTHER P88   Germany

Manufacturer: Carl Walther GmbH, Ulm/Donau, Germany

Although the P5 met with initial success, like all the P38 family it is, by modern standards, a difficult weapon to manufacture due to the method of breech locking which was adopted. Shortly after the P5 went on sale, newer designs from other manufacturers appeared which were less expensive, and sales of the P5 suffered. Walther therefore set about developing an entirely new pistol, the **P88** in an attempt to regain their market position.

The P88 appeared in 1988 and was a completely new design; the dropping wedge lock designed by Barthelmes in the 1930s was finally abandoned and the well-tried Colt/Browning method of locking the barrel to the slide and unlocking it by lowering the breech end by means of a cam was adopted for the first time. Instead of the usual ribs on the barrel locking into recesses in the slide, the chamber area of the barrel is formed into a rectangular shape, and this locks into the rectangular ejection port cut into the top of the slide; this method is easier

to manufacture than the rib system and is also a more positive lock, since guaranteeing complete engagement of the ribs involves very careful fitting.

The trigger mechanism is the familiar Walther double-action, and the firing-pin safety system is the same as that used on the P5, in which the pin is held out of alignment with the hammer by a

Right: The squared outline of the P88 was not typical of previous Walther pistols.

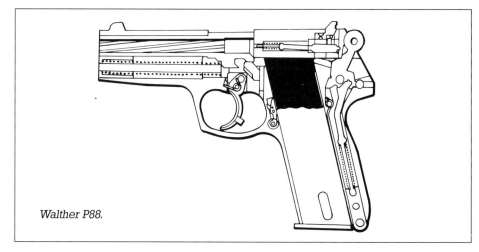

Walther P88.

spring until the final movement of the trigger linkage which lifts the pin into position. A de-cocking lever doubles as a slide release, and the magazine-release button is duplicated on both sides of the weapon. The sights are large and well-defined, and the rear sight is mounted on a screw base which allows it to be moved laterally for zeroing adjustment.

In addition to the standard 9mm Parabellum chambering, the P88 is available in 9x21mm, a 'compromise cartridge' that has been developed for sale in countries where 9x19mm (Parabellum) is restricted to military use.

The P88 has been tested by many countries, Britain included, but the near-collapse of Walther in the early 1990s has led to a rationalisation. The P88 is now available only in target-shooting configurations, prospects of military sales relying on the new **P99**. Already successfully licensed to Smith & Wesson, the P99 amalgamates the locking system of the P88 with extensive use of synthetic parts.

The P88 is a considerable departure from the earlier Walther designs, using a modified Browning tilting barrel to lock the breech. In the summer of 1993 a compact version was announced, with a 97mm barrel and 14-round magazine.

Specification:
Calibre: 9mm Parabellum
Operation: Short recoil, semi-automatic
Length: 187mm
Weight, empty: 900g

Barrel: 102mm, 6 grooves, right-hand twist
Magazine: 15-round box
Muzzle velocity: 350 m/sec

FÉG P9

Manufacturer: Fegyver és Gazkeszuelekgyara, Budapest (Variant Models: P9R; P9RA; FP9)

FÉG (the initials of a title which translates to 'Arms and Gas Appliances Factory') in their P9 series merely took the Browning GP-35 High-Power as it stood and copied it. There are some slight dimensional differences here and there, but in spite of this a high proportion of FÉG and Browning pieces are interchangeable. After this FÉG went on to introduce some improvements of their own and the variant models exhibit some interesting differences.

There is, therefore, no need to explain the P9 in great detail, since it simply duplicates the Browning GP-35. The first change to appear in the basic design was the adoption of a slide-mounted safety catch replacing the original frame-mounted pattern. This became the P9R and replaced the original P9 in production in the early 1980s. With it came the P9RA which has a light alloy frame, reducing the empty weight to 820 grammes. Both these weapons were provided with double-action triggers, a notable change from the original Browning design, and with ventilated sight ribs over the slide. The slide-mounted safety catch also acts as a de-cocking lever, lowering the hammer when applied and placing a positive block between the hammer and the safety pin; this mechanism has several affinities with that of the Walther P-38 pistol safety system. An interesting variation on the P9R is the availability of a completely left-handed version in which the safety catch, magazine release and slide stop lever are on the right side of the frame and the ejection port lies on the left side of the slide.

The original P9 is now known as the FP9, the principal change being a slight deepening of the frame in front of the trigger-guard and the addition of a ventilated sight rib. So far as is known no military force uses the P9 pistol, though it is believed that some European police forces have adopted them.

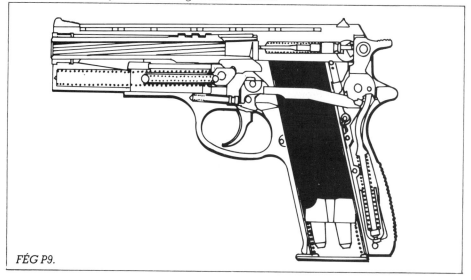

FÉG P9.

The FÉG P9 stripped for cleaning and showing its similarity to the Browning GP-35 design.

Right side of the FÉG FP9; slightly more angular and sharp-edged than the Browning GP-35, it also differs in having a ventilated rib on top of the slide, intended to prevent heat haze interfering with the sight line.

Specification:
Calibre: 9mm Parabellum
Operation: Short recoil, semi-automatic
Length: 203mm
Weight, empty: 1000g
Barrel: 118·5mm, 6 grooves, right-hand twist, one turn in 250mm
Magazine: 14-round box
Muzzle velocity: 350 m/sec

DESERT EAGLE

***Manufacturer: Ta'as Israel
Industries, Ramat Hasharon***

The **Desert Eagle** pistol was originally developed for long range target shooting and 'silhouette' shooting, but it has since been adopted by one or two Special Forces who require this particular type of firepower. It is a big, heavy pistol firing a powerful round, but it is not so grotesque as many specialised super-pistols and, with the proper cartridge, can be handled as well as most smaller pistols.

It can trace its ancestry back to the same Scandinavian design which fathered the Wildey gas-operated pistol, though the method of utilising the propellant gas to operate the **Desert Eagle** is much different to that of the Wildey. Both, however, use similar methods of locking the breech, a rotating bolt which is turned by a cam reacting with a stud fixed in the moving slide; the first rearward movement of the slide will rotate the bolt lock sufficient to unlock it, after which further slide movement draws the bolt back to extract and eject the spent case.

The gas action is provided by a short-stroke piston set in the frame beneath the barrel. In order to obtain a degree of delay before the piston moves, the gas port in front of the chamber directs the gas through a channel in the frame until it is almost beneath the muzzle; the gas is then directed downwards and back into the gas cylinder, where it strikes the piston. This strikes the forward part of the slide, which extends alongside and below the barrel and it drives the slide

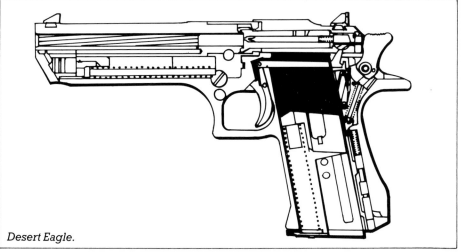

Desert Eagle.

backwards to start the unlocking of the breech. It will be seen that without the long and tortuous path of the gas channel, the breech would be likely to open far too quickly for safety; the alternative to this would be to make the moving parts a good deal heavier.

The **Desert Eagle** was unusual in being developed to fire a revolver cartridge, the ·357 Magnum. This choice was dictated by the desire to have a very powerful round which was easily obtainable almost anywhere in the world. The gun was later developed in ·44 Magnum calibre, making it rather more of a handful to control, and in 1989 it was announced that it would be made in ·41 Action Express calibre. This, it appears, was not enough for the seekers after the utmost power, and in 1992 it appeared chambered for the ·50 Action Express cartridge.

The Desert Eagle is a large and powerful pistol for long-range shooting; the upper surface of the barrel is grooved to mount a telescope sight and the iron sights can be either plain combat type or adjustable target pattern.

Specification:
Calibre: ·357 Magnum, ·44 Magnum, ·41 AE, ·50 AE
Operation: Gas, semi-automatic
Weight: 1·76kg
Length: 260mm
Barrel: 152mm, 6 grooves, right-hand twist
Magazine: 9-round magazine
Muzzle velocity: 450 m/sec.

JERICHO

**Manufacturer: Ta'as Israel
Industries, Ramat Hasharon**

Although from the same stable as the Desert Eagle this is a much different weapon, being aimed more at the military and security markets than the competition shooter. It is a conventional recoil-operated semi-automatic pistol, using a cam-dropped barrel to lock the breech; in fact it is more or less the CZ75 pistol as built by the Italian firm of Tanfoglio, reworked to give it a family resemblance to the Desert Eagle. Manufacture is divided between Tanfoglio and Ta'as Industries. The slide runs on rails inside the frame, a more expensive method of construction but one which is generally considered to give far better support to the slide and improve the accuracy of the pistol. The slide-mounted safety catch also acts as a de-cocking lever, and drops the hammer on to the locked firing pin when depressed. The safety catch is duplicated, so that it can be applied by either hand. Unusually for a modern design, there is no form of automatic firing pin safety system.

The **Jericho** is called the '941 Model' because of its unusual ability to change from 9mm to ·41 calibre very quickly. This combination has been chosen because the rim diameter of both cartridges is the same, so that only the barrel and magazine need to be changed to suit the new calibre. Replacement barrel, return spring and magazines are supplied with the pistol, and changing calibre is simply a matter of field-stripping the pistol and then re-assembling it with the replacement parts. The relevant parts are all colour-coded so that there is little risk of inadvertently assembling the wrong units.

The sights are the usual blade foresight and square notch rearsight; but, instead of the usual dots of white paint for use in poor light they are actually fitted with Tritium light inserts which give an excellent night sight picture, and one which will not fade away as the paint wears off. Both front and rear sights can be laterally adjusted.

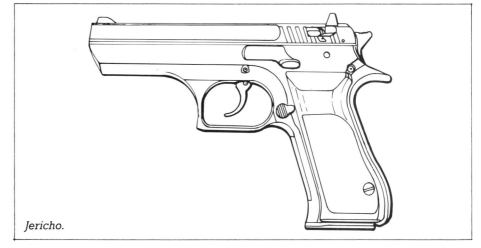

Jericho.

Specification:
Calibre: 9mm Parabellum or ·41 AE
Operation: Short recoil, semi-automatic
Length overall: 207mm
Weight, empty: 1·103kg
Barrel: 112mm, 6 grooves right-hand twist
Magazine: 16-round box (11-round in
·41 calibre)
Muzzle velocity: 350 m/sec.

Although the Jericho resembles the Desert Eagle, its mechanism is more conventional, using the familiar Browning tilting barrel to lock the breech.

The Jericho stripped into its basic parts for cleaning, with both the 9mm and ·41 barrels and their return springs.

45

UZI PISTOL

Israel

Manufacturer: Ta'as Israel Industries, Ramat Hasharon

The Uzi submachine gun is one of the classic designs, and well-known throughout the world. In the early 1980s the manufacturers decided to bow to the current fashion and make it somewhat more compact, developing the 'Mini-Uzi' and later the 'Micro-Uzi'. Inevitably, the question of firing these smaller weapons one-handed arose, and from that came the idea of turning the Mini-Uzi into a semi-automatic pistol.

Turning a submachine gun into a pistol involves a certain amount of re-design so that ill-intentioned people cannot turn it back into a submachine gun, and the interior of the **Uzi pistol** is considerably different to that of its ancestors. In the submachine gun the firing pin is a fixture in the bolt and fires the cartridge as the bolt is closing; in the pistol the firing pin is a separate unit attached to a plate at the rear of the bolt, so that as the block closes the plate is caught by the sear of the firing mechanism and held back against the pressure of the firing pin spring. The Uzi bolt is, like that of the submachine gun, a 'telescoped' bolt; the face of the

bolt is recessed so that when closed, half the bolt is surrounding the barrel. This enables the action to be shorter and more compact, while allowing the bolt to have the amount of weight necessary to resist the rearward thrust of the cartridge when it fires; for the **Uzi pistol** is a blowback weapon – there is no bolt lock other than the bolt's inertia.

The magazine fits into the pistol grip and, due to the 'telescoped bolt' design, this is the centre of balance, so that the pistol handles well in firing, though it is heavy. The standard

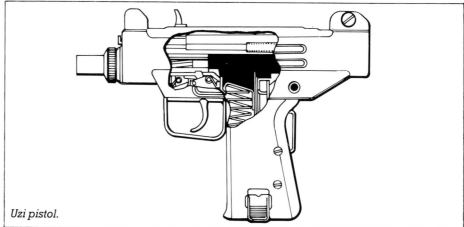

Uzi pistol.

magazine holds 20 rounds and, if desired, can be replaced by the submachine gun magazines which hold 25 or 32 rounds.

The sights are fully adjustable and have white reflective markers to assist aiming in poor light. Although appearances may be against it, the Uzi is quite capable of putting all its shots inside a 60mm circle at 25m range; this may not be Olympic standard but it is certainly good enough for military and security operations. And it is a good deal more robust than most pistols.

The Uzi pistol resembles the Uzi submachine gun but cannot be converted to automatic fire. The location of the magazine and butt at the point of balance makes it very easy to fire, in spite of its size and weight. The drawing (left) shows the pistol cocked, and shows the overhung element of the bolt above the chamber.

Specification:

Calibre: 9mm Parabellum
Operation: Blowback, semi-automatic
Weight: 1·81 kg
Length: 242mm
Barrel: 115mm, 4 grooves, right-hand twist
Magazine: 20-round box
Muzzle velocity: 335 m/sec.

BERETTA Model 951   Italy

Manufacturer: Pietro Beretta SpA, Gardone Val Trompia

The Beretta company have made pistols for the Italian armed forces since 1915, all of which were simple blowback weapons firing the 7·65mm ACP or 9mm Short cartridges. In their postwar re-organisation the Italian Army decided they wanted a more powerful weapon firing the near-universal 9mm Parabellum cartridge, and the **Beretta Model 951** was the result. Design work began in 1950 but was delayed because of a praise-worthy attempt to lighten the weapon by making the frame of light alloy. The result was a weapon which worked but which was unpleasant to shoot since the light weight resulted in an unacceptable level of recoil, and which had a potentially limited life since the force of the recoiling slide tended to damage the light frame. Eventually the design was re-worked with a steel frame; the additional weight made the weapon more controllable and the stronger metal precluded damage. The final version went into Italian service in 1957, and it was later adopted by the Israeli Army and others. It was adopted by Egypt and in

the 1960s a licensed copy, known as the **'Helwan'**, was manufactured in that country.

The **Model 951** is recoil-operated and the breech is locked by a wedge system similar to that first used in the **Walther P-38.** Like almost all Beretta pistols, the slide is cut away on top so as to expose most of the barrel, a short enclosed section at the front supporting the foresight. The wedge, which lies beneath the breech, locks the barrel to the side arms of the slide. On firing, barrel and slide recoil

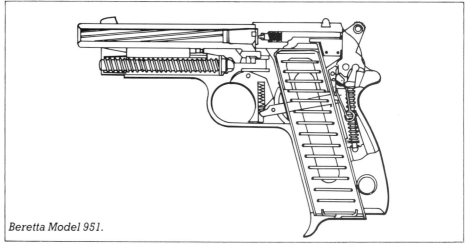

Beretta Model 951.

48

together for a short distance, sufficient time elapsing to allow the bullet to leave the muzzle and breech pressure to drop to a safe level. At that time the wedge, which carries a spring-loaded buffer, strikes a solid part of the frame and is deflected downwards, releasing the slide to continue its rearward movement to extract, eject and re-cock. On the forward stroke the fresh cartridge is loaded and the breech is closed; this forces the barrel forward, lifting the wedge so as to lock once more to the slide.

The trigger action is simple single-action, the weapon needing to be manually cocked before firing by pulling back the slide; the safety catch can then be applied and the pistol carried 'cocked and locked'.

The Model 951 was the first locked breech Beretta pistol and was adopted by the Italian, Egyptian, Israeli and Nigerian armies. Using the Walther P-38 locking block method of closing the breech, it acted as the test-bed for the design which later became the Model 92.

Specification:
Calibre: 9mm Parabellum
Operation: Short recoil, semi-automatic
Length overall: 203mm
Weight, empty: 890g
Barrel: 114mm, 6 grooves, right-hand twist
Magazine: 8-round box
Muzzle velocity: 350 m/sec

BERETTA Model 92   Italy

Manufacturer: Pietro Beretta SpA, Gardone Val Trompia

(Variant Models: 92F, 92F Compact, 92S, 92SB, 92SB-C, 92SB-C Type M, 98, 98F and 99)

The **Model 92** appeared in 1976 and might be thought of as being the **Model 951** brought up to date. The magazine capacity was increased and the trigger mechanism changed to double-action, but the general shape, the recoil operation and method of locking the breech are exactly the same as that used on the **951**.

The basic **Model 92** has led to a number of variations. Among the first was the **Model 92S**, in which the safety catch was moved from the frame to the slide and given a hammer de-cocking function. Pressing the safety catch releases the hammer after deflecting the firing pin out of the hammer path. Both the **92** and **92S** were adopted by the Italian armed forces and police and widely sold overseas before production ended in about 1986.

In 1980 the US Army sought a replacement for their Colt M1911A1 pistol and Beretta prepared the **Model 92SB** for their tests; this was a 92 with a safety catch on both sides of the slide,

the magazine release in front of the butt, behind the trigger, and an automatic firing pin safety system. The hammer had a half-cock notch and the butt was grooved at the rear to give a better grip. At the same time a 'compact' model, the **92SB-C** was developed, differing only in being smaller. The **Model SB** was successful but the US Army requested some modifications before adopting the design; the modified weapon became the **Model 92F** and the differences were slight. The trigger guard was re-

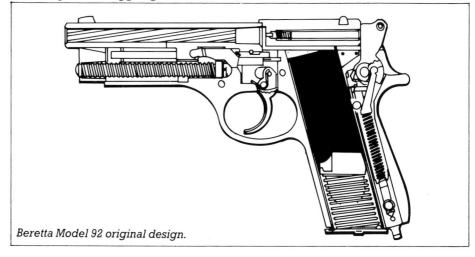

Beretta Model 92 original design.

50

shaped to suit a two-handed grip, the magazine had its base extended, the butt front edge was curved at the toe, and new grip plates and a lanyard ring were fitted. The barrel is chromed internally and the external finish is 'Bruniton', a Teflon-type material . The **92F** was also adopted by the French Gendarmerie and is the current production model.

The other variants can be disposed of fairly rapidly; the **92SB-C Type M** is an **SB-C** with an eight-round magazine; the **92F Compact** is the **92SB-C** with the **92F** modifications; the **98** is a **92SB-C** chambered for the 7·65mm Parabellum cartridge; and the **99** is a **92SB-C Type M** chambered for the 7·65mm Parabellum cartridge.

The Beretta 92 has undergone several changes since the original design shown in the drawing (left); above is the Model 92FS, the latest production version, which equips the US armed forces and Coastguard, the French Gendarmerie Nationale, the Italian Army and other armed forces throughout the world.

Specification:
Calibre: ·9mm Parbellum
Operation: Short recoil, semi-automatic
Length: 217mm
Weight, empty: 950g
Barrel: 125mm, 6 grooves, right-hand twist, one turn in 250mm
Magazine: 15-round box
Muzzle velocity: 390 m/sec.

BERETTA Model 93R

Manufacturer: Pietro Beretta SpA, Gardone Val Trompia

Although the **951A** was what the customer wanted, Beretta were not particularly happy with the design and had their own ideas of what a machine pistol ought to be. The principal objection to full-automatic pistols is their unavoidable tendency to muzzle climb due to the recoil force which means that only the first two or three rounds are in the target area. Beretta therefore dropped the full-automatic option and, instead, fitted a three-round burst limiting device. A selector switch on the frame allows the firer to select single shots, in which mode the **93R** is simply a rather larger version of the **92** and acts accordingly.

With the switch set for burst fire, each pressure of the trigger produces three shots at a cyclic rate of about 1100 rounds per minute. This is still rather difficult to control with one hand, so there is a folding forward grip attached to the elongated trigger guard so that the firer can use his free hand to hold the grip, hooking his thumb into the trigger guard, and thus have better directional control.

For even more deliberate firing a collapsible metal butt can be clipped to the end of the pistol's grip and the weapon can then be fired from the shoulder.

To assist in controlling the recoil the barrel is extended and the muzzle is formed into a compensator which also acts as a flash hider when firing at night. Extended magazines are available, giving an increased ammunition reserve; they also add useful weight which helps in

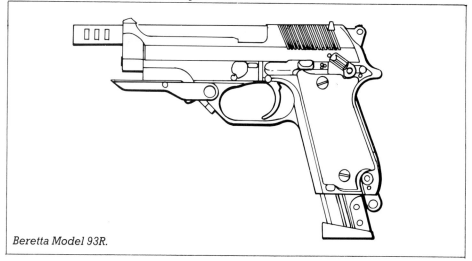

Beretta Model 93R.

52

controlling the weapon during burst fire.

The **Model 93R** has been adopted by the Italian Special Forces, replacing their earlier **951A** and **951R** models, and has also been purchased by Special Forces of other countries.

The Beretta 93R, showing the forward grip folded up under the frame and the detached metal shoulder stock which can be fitted for additional control. The selector lever on the slide allows single shots, three-round bursts or a safe position, and the muzzle compensator keeps muzzle rise to a minimum.

Specification:
Calibre: 9mm Parabellum
Operation: Short recoil, selective fire
Length overall: 240mm
Weight, empty: 1120g
Barrel: 156mm, 6 grooves, right-hand twist, one turn in 250mm
Magazine: 15-or 20-round box
Cyclic rate: 1100 rds/min
Muzzle velocity: 375 m/sec

Manufacturer: Tula arsenal

This was the outcome of trials undertaken in the 1920s to find a replacement for the 1895-type Nagant 'gas-seal' revolver. It was essentially an amalgamation of the 1903-type FN-Browning and the M1911 Colt-Browning, chambered for a variant of the 7.63mm Mauser pistol cartridge.

The first **TT30** ('Tula-Tokarev Model 1930') pistols were issued for field trials in 1931. They had tipping-barrel locks actuated by a swing-link, relying on two ribs formed on the barrel above the chamber to rise into recesses in the slide. Lips were machined in the frame above the magazine instead of relying on individually-shaped magazine bodies, partly in an attempt to improve the reliability of the feed and partly to avoid too much reliance on accurate sheet-metal work. The hammer and the trigger mechanism were contained in a detachable sub-assembly that could be removed from the frame for cleaning or repair, but the Tokarev lacked an applied safety of any type.

Experience with the trials guns

led to the **TT33**, with the locking ribs milled entirely around the circumference of the barrel and the back strap (previously separate) included in the frame forging. The absence of designation markings suggests that these improvements can be detected only by dismantling the guns, but the presence of a date on the slide usually provides an arbiter.

Series production began in 1936,

the guns being distinguished by plastic grips with roundels containing a five point star and 'CCCP'. Nagant revolvers continued to be made alongside the Tokarevs, for issue to the rank-and-file and the crews of tanks and armoured vehicles.

However, the Tokarev suffered so many teething troubles that trials with fixed-barrel pistols began in 1938. Work was still under way when

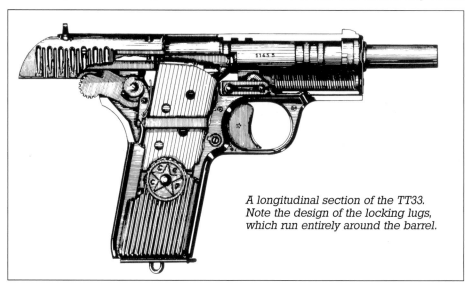

A longitudinal section of the TT33. Note the design of the locking lugs, which run entirely around the barrel.

the Germans invaded the Soviet Union in June 1941 and so the Tokarev went into full-scale production for the duration of hostilities. Wooden grips were used extensively during the Second World War, deterioration in the quality of finish and material reflecting the wholesale dislocation of Soviet industry in 1941–43.

Tokarevs were made in quantity in the USSR until 1953, and also in Hungary, Yugoslavia and the People's Republic of China. Consequently, many differing versions will be encountered. Among them are the standard 7.62mm Hungarian **48.M**; the Chinese 7.62mm **Types 51** and **54**; the Polish **Pistolet TT**; and the Yugoslavian 7.62mm **M57** and 9mm **M65**. The **Tokagypt**, made in Hungary in the 1950s for the Egyptian Army, is a variant of the TT that chambers the 9mm Parabellum cartridge and has a distinctive wrap-around wooden grip.

Specification (TT33):
Calibre: 7.62mm Tokarev
Operation: Short recoil, semi-automatic
Length: 195mm
Weight, empty: 822g
Barrel: 114mm, 4 grooves, right-hand twist
Magazine: 8-round box
Muzzle velocity: 457 m/sec

The standard Soviet-issue Tokarev TT33.

The Tokagypt, made in Hungary by FÉG, was a 9mm version of the Tokarev destined for the Egyptian Army.

Manufacturer: State arsenals

The **Makarov** pistol was developed in the early 1950s to replace the Tokarev TT-33 with something simpler to make and easier to shoot. Like all powerful pistols the Tokarev takes some training in order to extract the best from it, but the Makarov uses a much less powerful cartridge and is therefore more easily mastered. It became the standard sidearm for all Soviet forces, eventually replaced the Stechkin, and has been exported to many countries who have adopted Soviet weapons.

The design of the Makarov is broadly based upon that of the Walther PP, a fixed-barrel blowback semi-automatic with the recoil spring wrapped round the barrel. The trigger is double-action, and the safety catch, which is on the slide, locks the firing pin and lowers the hammer safely on to a loaded chamber when applied. Once this has been done, all that is necessary to fire is to release the safety catch and pull the trigger. This will cock the hammer and then release it to fire the first shot. Subsequent shots

will be fired in the single-action mode since the recoiling slide cocks the hammer after each shot.

It can be seen that the shape of the grip is much different to that of the Walther, which makes the Makarov somewhat awkward to hold for those accustomed to the PP; stripping is performed in the Walther manner, pulling the trigger guard down and forward to free the slide, after which the slide can be pulled all the way to the rear, the back end lifted clear of the frame, and then the slide can be slid forward, over the barrel, and removed.

The 9x18mm Makarov cartridge was introduced with this pistol and soon became a standard cartridge throughout the Warsaw Pact countries. It is somewhat smaller than the 9mm Parabellum but more powerful than the 9mm Short, so that it is just about at the upper limit of power which can be used in a simple blowback pistol. It is unfortunate that at much the same time the same sort of reasoning led to the development of a similar 9x18mm cartridge in the West; this is the 9mm Police round, which although of the same nominal

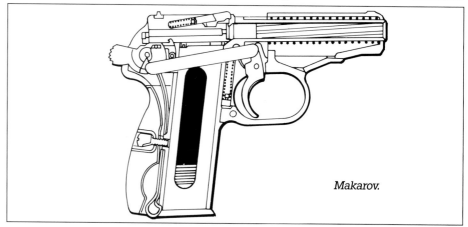

Makarov.

A typical Chinese-made Makarov.

dimensions is, in fact, very slightly different, so that Western weapons cannot chamber the Makarov cartridge and Soviet pistols cannot fire the 9mm Police round.

Though supplemented in the Soviet armed forces by the small-calibre PSM, the Makarov remains the rank-and-file service weapon of the Russian Army, and is still being made in Izhevsk for paramilitary, police and commercial customers. In addition, large quantities were made elsewhere in the Soviet bloc, most notably in the Sauer factory in Suhl in the former East Germany, in Bulgaria, and also in the People's Republic of China. These guns can usually be recognised by their markings.

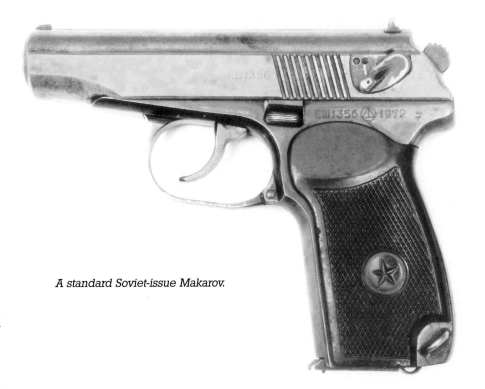

A standard Soviet-issue Makarov.

Specification:

Calibre: 9mm Makarov
Operation: Blowback, semi-automatic
Length: 160mm
Weight, empty: 663g

Barrel: 91mm, 4 grooves, right-hand twist
Magazine: 8-round box
Muzzle velocity: 315 m/sec

ASTRA 400 Spain

**Manufacturer: Unceta y Cia,
Guernica
(Now Astra-Unceta y Cia)
(Variant Model: Astra 600)**

The **Astra 400** is that remarkable oddity, a blowback pistol firing a heavy military cartridge. The 9mm Largo cartridge is longer than the 9mm Parabellum and uses a heavier bullet, but the velocity and the muzzle energy are lower. Nevertheless, it delivers considerable recoil and to keep the blowback system under control demanded a heavy return spring and hammer spring to soak up the energy. Cocking the **Astra** requires a very tight grip on the slide to overcome the powerful spring.

Another remarkable feature of this pistol is its ability, when new, to fire a number of different cartridges. It will, when in good condition, chamber and fire the 9mm Browning Long, 9mm Largo, 9mm Steyr and ·380 Colt Auto cartridges, and it manages this by a carefully dimensioned chamber and a long firing pin which absorbs small differences in headspace. Once the chamber begins to wear, this tolerance begins to vanish, and with the age of the pistols likely to be found today it is

not a practice to be recommended. The most usual problem arises when attempting to fire 9mm Parabellum in a worn gun; failures to feed often occur, and if they do feed, then they tend to go forward in the chamber so that they are not properly supported by the breech face and blow out their primers.

Production of the **Astra 400** ended in 1946, after some 106,000 had been made. During 1943 an interesting variant model, the **Astra 600,** was made for the German Army; this was a slightly smaller version of the 400 chambered specifically for the 9mm Parabellum cartridge. A total of 10,450 were delivered, after which a further 49,000 or so were made and marketed commercially. A number were supplied to West German police forces in the immediate postwar years.

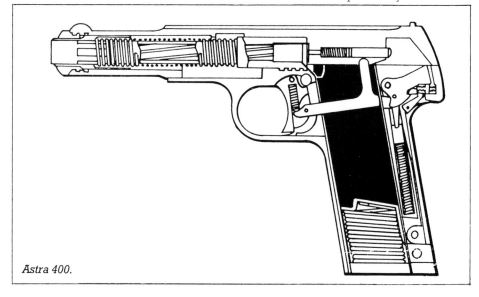

Astra 400.

58

Specification:
Cartridge: 9x23mm Largo (Bergmann-Bayard)
Operation: Blowback, semi-automatic
Length: 235mm
Weight, empty: 1080g
Barrel: 140mm, 6 grooves, right-hand twist
Magazine capacity: 8 rounds
Muzzle velocity: 345m/sec.

Though it may resemble an air pistol, the Astra 400 was a military weapon firing a powerful cartridge. The design is a modification of the Campo Giro pistol, adopted by the Spanish Army in 1912 and improved by Astra after the death of the inventor in 1915. Astra's design was put into service in 1921, approximately the date of this rare photograph, and was not replaced until the 1950s. The lower photograph shows the Astra 400 with its slide drawn back, showing how the slide fits concentrically around the barrel.

ASTRA A-80

**Manufacturer: Astra-Unceta y Cia,
Guernica
(Variant Model: Astra A-90)**

The Astra **A-80** is a semi-automatic pistol of modern design, especially adapted for police and military use. Its various features include an advanced double-action mechanism, large magazine capacity, compact size and a choice of popular calibres. The safety system permits carrying the pistol with a loaded chamber without danger of accidental discharge.

On the **A-80** the conventional manual safety catch on the slide is absent. Instead, the pistol has a de-cocking lever which operates in conjunction with the double-action trigger mechanism. Pressure on the de-cocking lever releases the hammer to allow a safety notch to engage with a corresponding notch on the sear, so arresting the hammer's movement before it can strike the firing pin. In addition, a safety block is automatically engaged in recesses in the firing pin, preventing the pin from moving, so that even should the sear fail and the hammer strike the pin, the cartridge will not fire.

The pistol can be fired from the full-cock or uncocked position by a pull of the trigger. In either case, the automatic firing pin safety block is raised, to free the firing pin, by the action of the sear during the final movement of the trigger. As normally supplied the pistol is designed for right-handed users, but a left-handed de-cocking lever and associated components can be provided.

The **A-80** was introduced in 1981 and has been purchased by a number of military and security forces. In 1985 an improved design, the **A-90** was introduced. This is much the same weapon but with the addition of a manual safety catch on the slide which is linked to a new two-piece firing pin. On setting the catch to safe the rear end of the firing pin is tilted so that the rear is concealed from the hammer and the front is no longer aligned with the rest of the pin. The de-cocking lever and automatic firing pin safety of the **A-80** are also present, so giving the user a number of safety options.

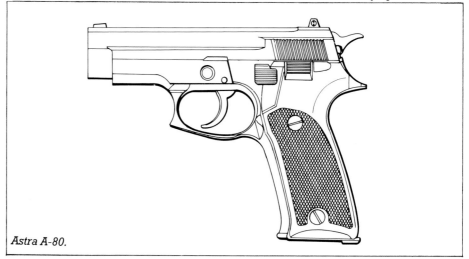

Astra A-80.

Specification:

Calibre: 9mm Parabellum, ·38 Super Auto, ·45 ACP or 7·65mm Parabellum
Operation: Short recoil, semi-automatic
Length: 180mm
Weight, empty: 985g
Barrel: 96·5mm
Magazine: 15-shot box (8-shot in ·45 calibre)
Muzzle velocity: 350 m/sec (9mm Parabellum)

Dismantling the Astra A-80 is done by rotating a locking pin and sliding the two halves of the pistol apart.

Reminiscent of the SIG-Sauer designs, the Astra A-80 uses a de-cocking lever to control its double-action firing mechanism. The later A-90 added a manual safety catch to the slide to give positive control over the firing pin.

LLAMA M82 Spein

Spain

Manufacturer: Llama-Gabilondo y Cia, Vitoria

Gabilondo began making cheap revolvers in 1904 and turned to simple automatic pistols during World War One in order to meet French demands. After the war they made copies of Browning pistols and then, in 1931, began producing the **'Llama'** series of automatics, which were among the best of Spanish pistols. These were all external-hammer single-action pistols based on the Colt M1911 design; they were well made and widely exported. The 9mm **'Llama Especial'** model was used by the Nationalist forces in the Spanish Civil War, and after that war Gabilondo were one the three Spanish gunmakers permitted to manufacture pistols (the others being Star-Bonifacio Echeverria and Astra-Unceta).

The **M82** was introduced in the early 1980s and was thereafter adopted by the Spanish Armed forces. It is a modern pistol, with double action trigger, and it moves away from the traditional Llama method of using the Browning lock to adopt a breech locking system relying upon a locking wedge beneath the barrel, the same system as pioneered on the Walther P-38. The wedge locks the barrel and slide together; as the two recoil after firing, so the wedge strikes a spring plunger mounted in the frame and is deflected downwards so as to unlock from the slide. The slide then performs the reloading cycle and is relocked to the barrel after the fresh round has been chambered.

The pistol is loaded in the usual way by setting the slide-mounted safety catch to 'safe' and inserting a magazine, then pulling back the slide and releasing it. As the slide goes forward so the hammer drops safely upon the loaded chamber. The pistol can then be carried, and when required all that is necessary is to push up the safety catch and pull the trigger.

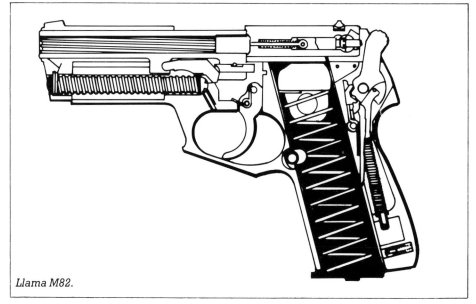

Llama M82.

Specification:
Calibre: 9mm Parabellum
Operation: Short recoil, semi-automatic
Length: 209mm
Weight: 1110g
Barrel: 114mm, 6 grooves, right-hand twist
Magazine: 15-round box
Muzzle velocity: 345 m/sec.

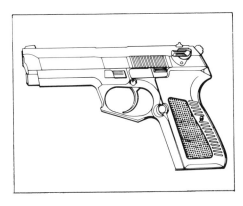

The Llama 82 is the current Spanish Army service pistol, and uses the same breech locking system as the Beretta 92. An unusual feature is that the hammer falls to a safe position after the gun has been loaded and the slide pulled back to load the chamber. It is possible to thumb-cock the hammer, but double-action shooting is the norm.

STAR Model 30M

**Manufacturer: Star Bonifacio
Echeverria SA, Eibar
(Variant Model: 30PK)**

The Star company are a long-established firm who have specialised in automatic pistols since the 1900s and who are one of the only three Spanish pistol makers to have survived the Civil War. In their early days the company appear to have taken Mannlicher as their design stimulus, but in the 1920s they adopted the familiar Colt/Browning pattern and have remained with it ever since.

The **Model 30** was introduced in 1988 and followed a Model 28, being an improvement on it. The design is modern in that it incorporates an automatic firing pin safety and has the safety catch duplicated on both sides of the slide to facilitate use by right- or left-handed firers. The barrel locking system is controlled by a cam beneath the breech end, acting against a pin in the frame to draw the rear end of the barrel down on recoil and so disengage it from the slide. Locking is performed by two ribs on the barrel mating with two recesses in the slide top.

An unusual feature in this pistol is that the slide is formed with an exterior flange which engages in a groove cut in the interior edge of the frame, so that the slide runs inside the frame; this has only previously been seen in Swiss pistols, and whilst it is doubtless more expensive to manufacture, it has the advantage of offering a longer support surface and thus keeping the slide and barrel assembly in more perfect alignment during the recoil stroke, adding to the accuracy of the weapon. The safety catch, when applied, retracts the firing pin into its housing so that it cannot be struck by the hammer.

Once the safety has been applied it is simply a matter of pulling the trigger to drop the hammer, after which the pistol can be carried in safety. To fire, the safety is released and the trigger pulled through in order to cock and release the hammer for the first shot. The manufacturers also claim that this system allows the firer to practice 'dry firing' with an empty pistol without the danger of damaging the firing pin. There is also a magazine safety system which prevents the trigger operating if the magazine has been removed; in recognition of the fact that some users dislike this device, it has been fitted in

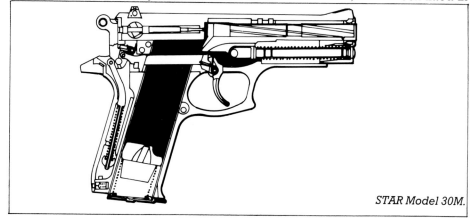

STAR Model 30M.

64

such a manner that the user can remove it if he wishes.

The **Model 30PK** is slightly smaller and has a light alloy frame.

Specification:

Calibre: 9mm Parabellum
Operation: Short recoil, semi-automatic
Weight: 1·14kg (30M); 860g (30PK)
Length: 205mm (30M); 193mm (30PK)
Barrel: 120mm (30M); 98mm (30PK)
Magazine: 15-round box
Muzzle velocity: 375 m/sec.

Standard pistol of the Spanish police services, the Star 30M is unusual in that it is possible to pull the trigger and actuate the hammer even when the safety catch is applied, since this only retracts the firing pin and locks it.
Left: a rear view of the Star 30M, showing the luminous dot sights.

SIG-SAUER P-220   Switzerland

Manufacturer: Schweizerische Industrie Gesellschaft (SIG), Neuhausen-Rheinfalls, J. P. Sauer & Sohn, Eckernförde, Germany

In the early 1970s, doubtless motivated by the various demands for modern automatic pistols which were being made by European police forces faced with increasing terrorism, SIG set out bringing their **P-210** design up to date, making it easier and therefore cheaper to manufacture and also adding some new features.

But no matter how good the pistol might be once put into production, the Swiss laws on the export of firearms had become very stringent, and it was likely that SIG would be unable to sell the weapon outside Switzerland, a market which scarcely made development worthwhile. They therefore set up an arrangement with J. P. Sauer & Sohn, an old-established firearms maker in West Germany, whereby SIG would develop the pistol and Sauer would then make it under license, the German regulations permitting much easier export sales. The result was that the new pistol was introduced as the **SIG-Sauer P-220**.

The **P-220** retains the dropping barrel method of locking the breech, but the method of locking the slide is much simpler; a squared block around the chamber fits into the enlarged ejection port in the side and does the locking. Instead of being machined from raw steel, the new design makes use of investment castings which are then machined on computer-controlled tools.

The trigger is double-action and there is a de-cocking lever on the left side of the frame, allowing the hammer to be lowered safely and then, if desired, cocked for single-action firing. There is an automatic firing pin lock which will only allow the pin to move when the trigger is correctly pulled. In view of these features SIG see no reason to have a manual safety catch on the pistol.

The **P-220** was adopted by the Swiss Army as their **Pistol 75**; it is also used by the Japanese Self-Defence Force and by a number of Special Forces.

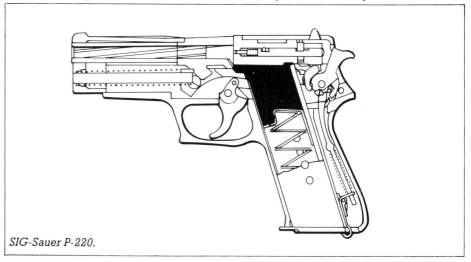

SIG-Sauer P-220.

Specification:

Calibre: 9mm Parabellum
Operation: Short recoil, semi-automatic
Length: 198mm
Weight, empty: 830g
Barrel: 112mm, 6 grooves, right-hand twist
Magazine: 9-round box
Muzzel velocity: 345 m/sec.

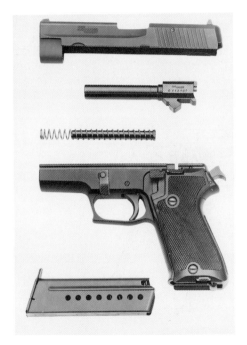

The SIG-Sauer P-220 heralded a new generation of SIG pistols when it appeared in 1974. The locking, by means of the chamber area into the ejection port, was unique, and the de-cocking lever resurrected a design used by Sauer in their 1938 pistol. Adopted by the Swiss and Japanese armies, it is widely used by security forces all over the world.
Left: this view of the SIG-Sauer P-220 dismantled shows the cam beneath the chamber and the shaped area around the chamber which provides the breech locking.

SIG-SAUER P-225 & P-226   Switzerland

Manufacturer: Schweizerische Industrie Gesellschaft (SIG), Neuhausen-Rheinfalls, J. P. Sauer & Sohn, Eckernförde, Germany.

The P-220 was a considerable success, and led to requests for something similar but rather smaller, which could be carried concealed. This led to the **SIG-Sauer P-225**, which took the basic design of the P-220 and simply reduced its dimensions and weight. The automatic firing pin safety was improved so that not only did it keep the pistol safe against accidental discharge, it also prevented discharges due to the pistol being dropped or struck whilst cocked.

The **P-225** appeared shortly after the German Federal Police authority had specified various features for a new pistol, and since it complied with most of these requirements it was soon adopted by a number of Swiss and German state police forces. It was also taken into use by the US Secret Service, and a number of Special Forces of different armies have adopted it.

In 1980 the US Army made its requirements for a new pistol known, and SIG saw that with some small modifications the **P-225** could be a likely contender. Using many existing parts of the P-220 and P-225, they developed the **P-226** and submitted it for the US Army trials. The pistol was almost the same size as the P-220 but adopted a larger capacity magazine and an ambidextrous magazine release in order to meet American requirements.

The **P-226** did extremely well in the US trials and was rated a 'technically acceptable finalist'; indeed, it was widely believed that it would be chosen as the US Army's new pistol, arrangements having been made for manufacture in the USA by the Maremont Corporation. However, at the last moment it was beaten on price by the Beretta 92F, which was duly accepted by the US Army. In spite of this setback SIG put the **P-226** into production and it has been adopted by several military and police forces throughout the world.

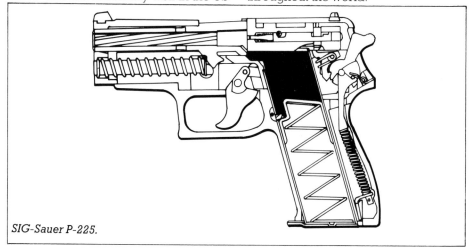

SIG-Sauer P-225.

68

Specification (P-225):
Calibre: ·9mm Parbellum
Operation: Short recoil, semi-automatic
Length: 180mm
Weight, empty: 740g
Barrel: 98mm, 6 grooves, right-hand twist
Magazine: 8-round box
Muzzle velocity: 340 m/sec.

Specification (P-226):
Calibre: ·196mm
Weight, empty: 750g
Barrel: 112mm, 6 grooves, right-hand twist
Magazine: 15-round box
Muzzle velocity: 350 m/sec.

The SIG-Sauer P-225 (above) is a smaller version of the 220 with even more safety devices, so that even if the hammer slips during cocking it remains perfectly safe. There is no safety catch, and operation is as instinctive as that of a revolver. The P-226 (left) is a variant model designed to compete in the US pistol trials of 1981, in which it was narrowly beaten on price by the Beretta 92.

SIG-SAUER P-228 Series Switzerland

Manufacturer: Schweizerische Industrie Gesellschaft (SIG), Neuhausen-Rheinfalls, J.P. Sauer & Sohn GmbH, Eckernförde, Germany
(Variants: P-228, P-229, P-229SL, P-239)

The **P-228** was developed to provide a compact pistol with a large magazine capacity, thus filling a gap in the SIG product line that had been exploited by rivals such as FN Herstal and Beretta. The P-228 has a double-action trigger system, a magazine capacity of 13 rounds, and has been specifically designed to resist the effects of dust and dirt.

An automatic firing-pin safety system and a de-cocking lever are standard, and the magazine catch can be mounted on either side of the frame. The P-228 shares many of the components of the P-225/P-226 series, and most of the accessories supplied with the earlier guns can also be used with the P-228.

The **P-229** (which has now replaced the standard P-228) is little more than a P-228 chambered for the .357 Auto or .40 S&W cartridges, though 9mm Parabellum has now become an option. It has been designed primarily for use by police and security forces, particularly in the USA where the .40 cartridge has attracted a considerable following.

There are three variant models: the basic P-229 has a steel slide and an aluminium frame, whereas the **P-229SL** has a stainless steel slide and frame. The 'SL' variant can also be supplied in 9mm Parabellum. The **P-239** is an improved compact version of the P-229, available with conventional single/double-action or double-action-only trigger systems.

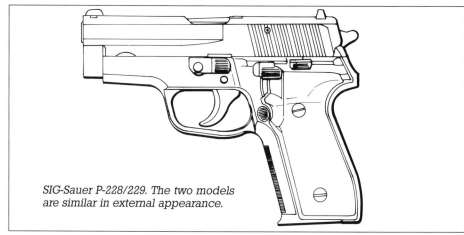

SIG-Sauer P-228/229. The two models are similar in external appearance.

Chambered for 9mm Parabellum, .357 Auto or .40 S&W, it is 168mm long and has a single-row magazine.

Specification (P-228):
Calibre: 9mm Parabellum
Operation: Short recoil, semi-automatic
Length: 180mm
Weight, empty: 830g
Barrel: 98mm, 6 grooves, right-hand twist
Magazine: 13-round box
Muzzle velocity: 340 m/sec

Specification (P-229):
Calibre: .40 Smith and Wesson
Operation: Short recoil, semi-automatic
Length: 180mm
Weight, empty: 865g
Barrel: 98mm, 6 grooves, right-hand twist
Magazine: 12-round box
Muzzle velocity: 290 m/sec

Based on a well-tried design, the P-228 is a compact pistol widely used by security forces and bodyguards in many countries.

SPHINX AT-2000S   Switzerland

**Manufacturer: Sphinx Engineering
SA, Porrentruy
(Variant Models: AT-2000P,
AT-2000H)**

This first appeared in 1984 as the ITM
AT-84 and was simply a licensed copy
of the Czech CZ75 made in
Switzerland. Thereafter the Swiss
licensees made a number of minor
changes and improvements, so that the
present **AT-2000** models can be
considered as individual designs in
their own right.

The barrels are specially made by a
specialist barrel-maker in Germany.
Several parts have been redesigned
so that they are now no longer interchangeable with original CZ75 parts. A
new Swiss-designed automatic firing
pin safety system has been added; this
keeps the firing pin positively locked
against any movement except during
the final stages of trigger pull. As soon
as the trigger is released, the safety
block returns to position and locks the
firing pin. Other improvements include
the duplication of the safety catch and
slide stop lever on both sides of the
frame, and the safety catch operating
system has been changed so that it can
be applied when the hammer is
cocked or uncocked.

The standard chambering is for 9mm
Parabellum, but the pistol can also be
supplied in 9x21mm calibre for those
countries where 9mm Parabellum is
forbidden to civilian shooters, or in ·40
Smith & Wesson calibre.

The **AT-2000S** is the standard model,
adopted by several police forces and
some military units. The **AT-2000P** is
a compact version, 184mm long and
weighing 940 grams, with all the
features of the **AT-2000S**. The
AT-2000H is the 'Hideaway' version,

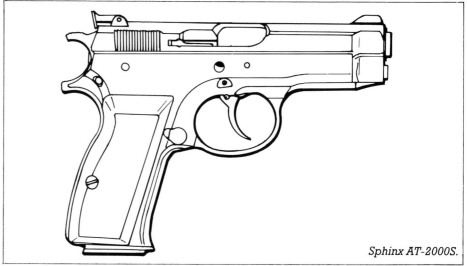

Sphinx AT-2000S.

even smaller and with a newly designed barrel and slide, but otherwise retaining all the standard features. As well as the three standard calibres, the **AT-2000H** is also available in 9mm Action Express calibre; this is a cartridge made from the ·41 AE case necked down to take a 9mm bullet, so giving more powder capacity in the case and allowing a higher velocity.

The Sphinx AT-2000 is one of many derivatives from the Czech CZ75, though sufficient changes have been made to turn it into an entirely new design. This Model PR is the most recent version, has a 'double-action only' firing mechanism, though the hammer can be thumb-cocked if desired.
Left: a stainless steel version of the Sphinx AT-2000S pistol.

Specification (AT-2000S):
Calibre: 9mm Parabellum, 9x21mm or ·40 S&W
Operation: Short recoil, semi-automatic
Length: 204mm
Weight, empty: 1030g
Barrel: 115mm, 6 grooves, right-hand twist, one turn in 250mm
Magazine: 15-round box (11-round in ·40 calibre)
Muzzle velocity: 352 m/sec.

CALICO M950   USA

**Manufacturer: Calico Inc.,
Bakersfield, USA**

The **Calico** appeared in 1989 and is a quite unusual weapon; it is modular in construction so that the various parts can be put together so as to produce either pistols or carbines, and the magazine is a tubular component which sits on top of the weapon and has an enormous capacity. Unlike any other pistol, the **Calico M950** feeds from above and ejects the spent cases below.

The frame and receiver unit of the **Calico** is made from cast aluminium and incorporates the butt and also a fore-end which can be grasped by the free hand for better control. The barrel is of chrome molybdenum steel. The bolt mechanism is a delayed blowback design similar to that used in the Heckler & Koch weapons; it consists of two parts, separated by two rollers. On closing, the rear (heavy) section forces the rollers outwards into two recesses formed in the frame. On firing, the rearward thrust on the face of the bolt tries to force the entire bolt assembly rearwards, but movement is prevented because of the engagement of the rollers. The lighter front section

of the bolt is allowed a small amount of movement, and this is enough to allow shaped faces to slowly force the rollers inward until they cease to have any locking effect. At that point the entire bolt unit is able to move back under the impetus given to the front section. The bolt travels back in the receiver, extracting and ejecting the empty case and compressing a return spring. A hammer is also cocked during this movement. The spring then returns the bolt, loading a fresh round, and the rollers move out to lock.

The magazine is a cylindrical casing which slides on to the rear of the receiver. Inside it, the cartridges are stacked in two helical layers, and as the rounds feed forward under pressure from a driving spring they roll so as to generate little friction. The standard magazine holds 50 rounds, but a longer magazine holding 100 rounds can also be fitted.

The rear sight is a notch on the magazine, and the front sight forms part of the frame and is fully adjustable for elevation and windage.

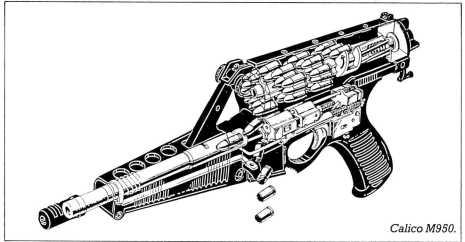

Calico M950.

Right: the Calico pistol is an unusual weapon, giving enormous firepower in one hand. This shows the pistol with the 50-round magazine in place, and the 100-round magazine above it.

Left: this drawing of the Calico shows the helical ammunition feed.

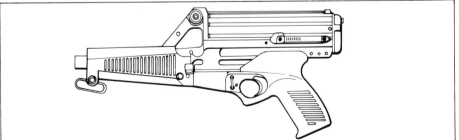

Specification:
Calibre: 9mm Parabellum
Operation: Delayed blowback, semi-automatic
Weight: 1·02kg empty
Length: 355mm with 50-round magazine
Barrel: 152mm, 6 groove, right-hand twist
Magazine: 50- or 100-round helical
Muzzle velocity: 393 m/sec

**Manufacturer: Colt's Patent Fire
Arms Mfg Co., Hartford,
Connecticut; and others
(Variant Model: M1911)**

Adopted by the US Army in March
1911, this is the most successful and
longest-lived automatic pistol design
in military history. It was based on
patents granted to John Browning in
1897–1909, protecting the method of
locking the breech with a 'swinging
link'.

The original design relies on two
links that swing the barrel down and
back, parallel to the axis of the bore.
The perfected version of this system,
the M1905, was tested extensively
against guns such as the Luger and
the Savage, eventually emerging
victorious once a change had been
made to a single link.

When the pistol is ready to fire, two
lugs on the top of the barrel above
the chamber engage recesses cut in
the undersurface of the slide; the
front of the barrel is supported in a
bush at the front of the slide, and the
rear of the barrel is held up by a
pivoting link that is attached to the
barrel at its upper end and to the
slide-stop pin at its lower end.

When the **M1911** fires, recoil
moves the barrel and slide backwards. As the barrel goes back, it
begins to pivot the actuating link
around the slide-stop pin and the top
of the link, which describes an arc,
pulls the rear of the barrel down until
the locking lugs disengage the slide.
The barrel then comes to a halt, but
the slide continues to move back,
allowing the extractor to pull the
empty case from the chamber, the
spent case to be ejected, and the
hammer to be cocked.

At the end of the recoil stroke, a
return spring beneath the barrel,
compressed during the opening
movement, expands to drive the
slide forward. This action strips a
fresh cartridge out of the magazine
and into the chamber; allows the link
to swing the rear of the barrel back
up and into engagement with the
slide; and runs the locked parts back
into battery. The hammer remains
cocked and the pistol is ready to fire
again.

A manual safety catch lies on the
frame, and a grip safety (in the form
of a movable plate) is let into the rear

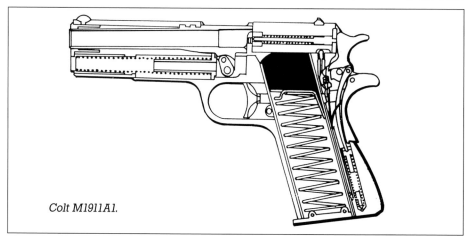

Colt M1911A1.

of the butt. Unless the hand grips the butt securely enough to release the grip safety, the weapon cannot be fired.

The M1911 was very successful, but the beginning of the First World War found guns in short supply. Though Colt and Springfield Armory had been making them in quantity, both were too busy with other projects to concentrate on it. Orders were placed with a variety of gun-making companies, including the Remington Arms–Union Metallic Cartridge Co., and some businesses, such as Lanston Monotype, with no prior experience of firearms. However, only Remington had delivered any 1911-type Colt-Brownings by the end of the war.

Combat experience suggested a number of changes, resulting in 1926 in the approval of the **M1911A1**. The rear of the butt was more curved; the front edge of the butt was chamfered behind the trigger; the hammer spur was shortened; and the trigger was made slightly smaller and grooved for a better grip.

Production was confined to Colt until the USA went to war in 1941, when the problems that had been evident in 1917 recurred. The solution was identical: recruit new manufacturers. The principal

Right: An original Remington-made M1911 pistol.

Below right: A Brazilian copy of the M1911A1, chambered for the 9mm Parabellum cartridge.

participants were Remington-Rand, the Ithaca Gun Co., and Union Switch & Signal Co.

The M1911A1 served the US Army until replaced in 1985 by the 9mm Pistol M9 (Beretta 92F), though there were – and still are – many commentators prepared to champion the older design. It is ironic that new versions of the Colt-Browning should have had such an impact on the commercial market in the last decade, and also that a gradual move away from 9mm Parabellum to .40 S&W and other cartridges is also beginning to influence military minds in the USA.

1911-type Colt-Browning pistols have been made in Norway (some Pistolen 657 (n) being pressed into German service during the Second World War) and Argentina; M1911A1-type guns have been made in Argentina, Brazil, Cambodia, the Philippines and the People's Republic of China in addition to the USA. Most of these variants can be identified by their slide markings.

Specification (M1911A1):
Calibre: .45 ACP
Operation: Short recoil, semi-automatic
Length: 216mm
Weight, empty: 1130g
Barrel: 127mm, 6 grooves, left-hand twist, one turn in 406mm
Magazine: 8-round box
Muzzle velocity: 253 m/sec

Mark 23 Mod 0 USA

Manufacturer: Heckler & Koch GmbH, Oberndorf/Neckar

In 1990 the US Special Operations Command (SOCOM) requested proposals for an automatic pistol in .45 calibre which was to be of superior accuracy to the M1911A1 and be provided with an accessory silencer and a laser aiming spot projector. Colt and Heckler & Koch both produced designs, and the latter was selected for development in 1991. Prototypes were tested in 1992–93, and a production contract was awarded in 1994. A total of 1380 pistols was purchased at a price of $1186 each. A similar number of silencers was bought from Knight's Armament Company, and 650 laser aiming projectors were also ordered.

The SOCOM pistol is generally similar to the Heckler & Koch USP which formed the basis of the design. It is a double-action design, hammer fired, with the breech locked by the Browning dropping barrel system. An additional recoil buffer is incorporated into the buffer spring assembly to reduce the felt recoil and thus improve the accuracy. The muzzle protrudes from the slide

and is threaded to accept the silencer (or sound suppressor), which is said to give a reduction of 25dB in noise. A slide lock is provided so that the pistol can be fired without the slide recoiling when the silencer is fitted, so that the noise of the slide and the ejected

cartridge do not negate the silencing of the shot. The front of the frame is grooved to accept the laser spot projector, which can project either visible or infra-red light. The use of infra-red light allows shooting in the dark by a man wearing night vision goggles, without revealing the

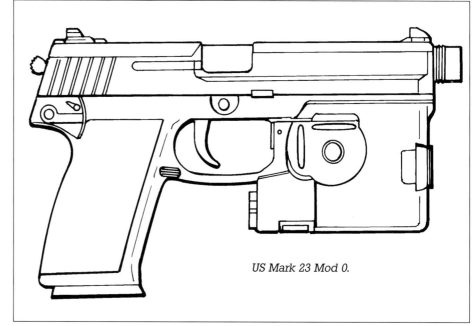

US Mark 23 Mod 0.

light to opponents (unless, of course, they are wearing NV goggles as well). The normal iron sights are also fitted with three tritium markers for aiming in poor light.

Specification:

Calibre: .45in
Operation: Recoil, dropping barrel
Length: 245mm; with suppressor, 421mm
Weight, empty: 1210g; with suppressor and full magazine, 1920g
Barrel: 149mm, 4 grooves, polygonal, right-hand twist
Magazine: 12-round detachable box
Muzzle velocity: approx. 270 m/sec (using M1911 ball)

With the accessories removed the origins of the Mark 23 Mod 0 in the Heckler & Koch USP are more apparent.

RUGER P85

Manufacturer: Sturm, Ruger & Co, Southport, Connecticut

Sturm, Ruger & Co came into existence shortly after World War Two producing an excellent .22 automatic pistol. Later, when the 'fast draw' craze swept the USA and Colt, ignoring it, failed to put their Single Action Army revolver back into production, Ruger began making single-action revolvers, and followed that by modern double-action weapons for police and security use. Rifles and shotguns were added, and finally, in the early 1980s, spurred no doubt by the US Army's demand for a new pistol, development of the **Ruger 85** began. Unfortunately it appeared too late for the US Army's trials, but in spite of that it has met with great success in civilian and police hands.

The Ruger 85 is in the modern idiom – a double-action pistol with the safety catch and magazine release duplicated on both sides so that it can be used equally easily by right- or left-handed firers. The frame is of light alloy and the remainder of high-grade steel, and extensive use has been made of precision investment casting for the manufacture. Originally located in New England, the company built a new plant, with modern computer-controlled machine tools, in Arizona to manufacture the Model 85.

The slide-mounted safety catch controls both the hammer and the firing pin; moving the catch to the safe position secures the firing pin and then drops the hammer safely.

Right: The Ruger P-85 field stripped to reveal its simple, robust and reliable design.

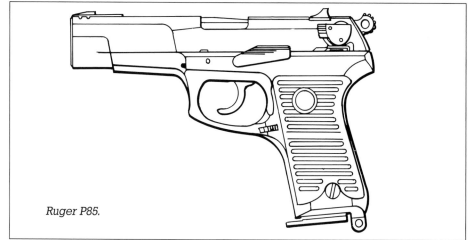

Ruger P85.

To fire, all that is required is to release the safety and pull the trigger; subsequent shots are in single-action mode. The trigger guard is larger than usual, allowing easy use by a gloved hand, and the front edge is shaped for a two-handed grip.

The pistol works by short recoil in the usual Colt/Browning way, the barrel being lowered by a shaped cam beneath the breech. The chamber section is squared off and locks into the ejection opening, a sturdy construction that is easier to make than the older rib-and-recess method.

The **P89** followed in 1989, together with a short-lived single-action derivative, for those (and there are many) who prefer their automatics in this form. Then came the **P89D**, with a de-cocking lever, and the double-action-only **P89DAO**.

Ruger has since made a large number of variations of the basic theme. These include the **P90** (.45 ACP), with an additional manual safety; the **P90D**, a P90 with an additional de-cocking capability; and the **P91D** (10mm Auto). The **P93** is a 9mm semi-compact version, 184mm long, available in 'D' or 'DAO' forms; the **P94** (standard, 'D' or 'DAO')

Arriving just too late for the US Army's pistol trials of the early 1980s, the Ruger P-85 has nevertheless found a place in the commercial market. There are now several variations in several calibres.

is a 9mm Parabellum/.40 S&W gun with an overall length of 190mm. The **P95** ('safety model', 'D', 'DAO') is strengthened for high-pressure 9mm Parabellum '+P+' ammunition, whereas the **P97** ('D' and 'DAO' only) is chambered for the .45 ACP round and has a single-column magazine.

Specification (P85):
Calibre: 9mm Parabellum
Operation: Short recoil, semi-automatic
Length: 200mm
Weight: 910g
Barrel: 114mm
Magazine: 15-round box
Muzzle velocity: 354 m/sec

S&W MODEL 29

Manufacturer: Smith & Wesson, Springfield, Mass.
(Variant Model: 629)

Horace Smith and Daniel Wesson met in the 1850s and as soon as Colt's master patent on revolvers expired in 1857 they went into production with the first breech-loading cartridge revolver, since which time, as they say, the company has never looked back. Their revolvers have always been made to a high standard of finish and are notable for their smooth trigger action. Comparisons with Colt are perhaps inevitable, but in truth there is little to choose between them from the mechanical point of view, one's choice is entirely a matter of personal preference.

The **Model 29** was, for some time, considered to be the most powerful handgun available, and it achieved considerable notoriety in the films of Clint Eastwood. It is a large and heavy weapon, necessarily so since it fired the ·44 Magnum cartridge, propelling a 15·5 gram bullet at 450 metres per second to deliver some 1150 foot-pounds of energy. The recoil from such a load is considerable, even with the weight of the pistol to soak some of

it up, and for many people the ·44 Model 29 is 'too much gun', which eventually led to the development of the ·41 Magnum cartridge and the Model 57 revolver, somewhat less of a handful.

The **Model 29** uses the large 'N' frame and locks the cylinder in place by the usual method of a spring-loaded central pin which anchors it securely to the standing breech and to a shroud formed beneath the barrel to accept the ejector rod. The hammer is chequered on its spur, and the trigger is grooved, both in order to give a non-

slip surface to obviate accidents. The rear sight is adjustable for windage, and the grips are somewhat thicker than usual in order to offer a full bearing surface for the hand and also to prevent the recoil force trapping a finger placed tightly behind the trigger guard or jarring the web of the thumb against the rear of the grip. There are four barrel lengths available – 102, 152, 213 and 260mm – and the pistol can be blued or nickel-plated. The **Model 629** is identical but is made entirely of stainless steel with a satin finish.

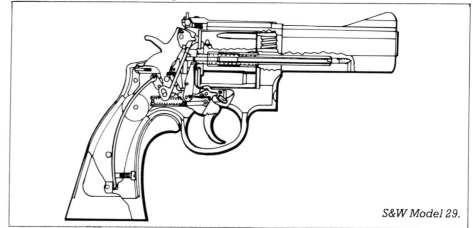

S&W Model 29.

Right: the Smith & Wesson Model 629 in stainless steel and with 4-inch barrel; other barrel lengths are 6·5 and 8·375 inch. With the longest barrel, the pistol weighs 51·5 ounces. The drawing (left) illustrates the robust mechanism, particularly the method of locking the cylinder into the frame.
Below: with the eight-inch barrel, the Model 29 is a lot of gun.

Specification (213mm barrel model):

Calibre: ·44 Magnum
Operation: Double-action revolver
Weight: 1·46kg
Length: 353mm
Barrel: 213mm, 6 grooves, right-hand twist
Magazine: 6-shot cylinder
Muzzle velocity: 450 m/sec.

S&W MODEL 5900 USA

Manufacturer: Smith & Wesson, Springfield, Mass.

Apart from a small pocket pistol in the 1920's, Smith & Wesson did little work on automatic pistols until the early 1950s, when they introduced the Model 39. This was a double-action 9mm automatic using the Colt/ Browning system of dropping barrel to lock the breech and slide together. It was provided with a manual safety catch on the slide and used a light alloy frame. It was gradually improved over the years and numbers were adopted by US Special Forces and the US Navy. In 1988 a new series of pistols, the 'Third Generation', was announced. Designed after consultation with many US military and police authorities, this series features such improvements as fixed barrel bushings for better accuracy, a greatly improved trigger-pull, three-dot sights for better aiming in poor visibility, a bevelled magazine aperture to make magazine changing quicker and easier, and improved safety features.

The Model 5900 is the full-sized 9mm Parabellum member of the series; it is accompanied by the mid-sized 3900 and compact 6900 models. The 5900 comes in three forms, the 5903 with alloy frame and steel slide, the 5904 with alloy frame and carbon steel slide, and the entirely stainless 5906: the other members of the series are similarly subdivided.

The double-action trigger mechanism is fitted with a manual safety and de-cocking lever mounted on both sides of the slide. This operates in the usual way, safely locking the firing pin before allowing the hammer to drop to the uncocked position. In addition, there is an automatic firing pin safety system in which a spring-loaded plunger positively locks the firing pin except during the final movement of the trigger in firing, when a pawl lifts the plunger and frees the pin to be struck by the falling hammer. Finally there is a magazine interlock safety which prevents the pistol being fired unless the magazine is in place.

The 9mm 5900 series is accompanied by the ·45in Model 4506. This is only

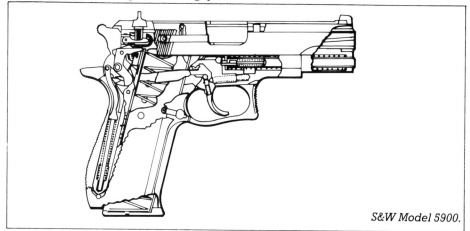

S&W Model 5900.

available as a stainless steel model and whilst larger in all dimensions than the 9mm pistols is to exactly the same design with the same features.

Specification:
Calibre: 9mm Parabellum
Operation: Short recoil, semi-automatic
Weight: 737g (Model 5904)
Length: 191mm
Barrel: 102mm, 6 grooves, right-hand twist
Magazine: 14-round box
Muzzle velocity: 350 m/sec.

The Smith & Wesson Model 5904, with alloy frame and steel slide, is representative of the S&W 'Third Generation' automatic models.
Left: the Smith & Wesson Model 1076 is a special 10mm model developed for use by the FBI.

PARKER-HALE MODEL 85

Manufacturer: Gibbs Rifle Co. Inc., Martinsburg, West Virginia, USA

The Parker-Hale company has been famous in the target-shooting world for many years, and the **Model 85** embodies all their experience in a weapon which is widely used by military and police authorities around the world. But in 1990 Parker-Hale sold its rifle business to the Gibbs Rifle Company of the USA, and the **Model 85**, and other Parker-Hale designs, are now manufactured there.

The **Model 85** uses a Mauser-type bolt action. The receiver is a one-piece machined forging into which the heavy barrel is screwed. The barrel is cold-hammered, giving additional strength and a high resistance to wear due to the work-hardening of the interior during the hammering process. It is assembled into the stock so that it is fully-floating, and is bedded into the stock with a special epoxy resin. The muzzle is counterbored to prevent any damage to the rifling when cleaning, and is threaded to accept the foresight block and a sound suppressor.

The bolt has frontal lugs which lock into the chamber, and there is an additional rear lug which, as the bolt is rotated to unlock, moves over a cam surface and eases the bolt back to give primary extraction. The trigger mechanism is a self-contained unit which is secured into the receiver by pins and can be completely removed for cleaning or adjustment. The single-stage trigger is carefully set at the factory for a short and crisp pull, but is fully adjustable by the user.

The safety catch is silent in operation and is of a unique design which positively locks the bolt, trigger and sear. The butt is adjustable for length and a quickly detachable and fully adjustable bipod is fitted to the fore-end. The rifle is fitted with a built-in aperture rear sight, adjustable to 900 metres range, and also has a dovetail to which telescope sights or passive night vision sights may be fitted.

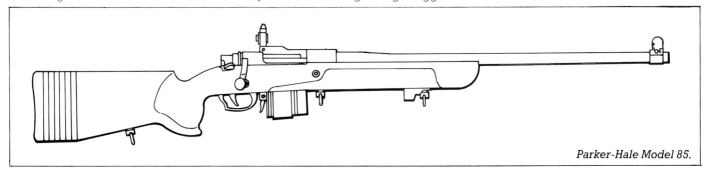

Parker-Hale Model 85.

The Parker-Hale Model 85 is a high-precision sniping rifle, seen here fitted with an electro-optical image intensifying night sight. With selected ammunition it is capable of giving first-round hits at all ranges up to 600 metres.

Specification:
Calibre: 7·62mm NATO
Operation: Manual single shot
Length: 1150-1210mm
Weight, empty: 5·70kg with telescope
sight
Barrel: 700mm, 4 grooves, right-hand twist
Magazine: 10-round box
Muzzle velocity: 860 m/sec.

STEYR AUG

Austria

Manufacturer: Steyr-Mannlicher GmbH, Steyr

AUG stands for 'Armee Universal Gewehr' and comes from the design of the weapon. It is an assault rifle which is constructed from a combination of modules, so that by changing various of these modules it can be configured as a carbine, assault rifle, infantry rifle or light machine gun. It was adopted by the Austrian Army in 1977 and since that time had gone into service in Australia, New Zealand, Ireland, Morocco, Saudi Arabia, Oman and Indonesia.

The basic rifle consists of a plastic stock into which slides a receiver unit carrying the bolt and gas operating system. The receiver is formed into a carrying handle which encloses a 1·5× optical sight. Into the front of the receiver fits the barrel, which locks in by a part-turn and has a carrying handle and also has a connection to the gas operating system. The transparent plastic magazine fits into the stock,

behind the grip since this is a 'bullpup' rifle with the barrel set well back in the stock so as to allow a full-length barrel in a compact overall size. Finally, the firing mechanism module slides into the rear of the stock and is retained in place by the butt plate.

It will be apparent from this description that changing the barrel is a simple movement, so that any barrel length can be fitted; the longest barrel is also heavier than standard, allowing sustained fire in the machine gun role.

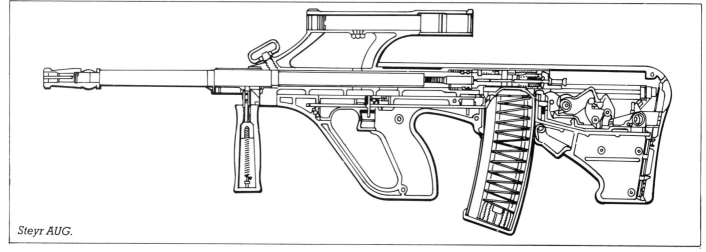

Steyr AUG.

The receiver can be changed; instead of one with the carrying handle and optical sight, a receiver with a telescope sight mount can be fitted and thus the user can then fit whatever sight he prefers to use. In standard form the firing mechanism allows single shots or automatic fire, controlled by the trigger; a light pull fires a single shot, but pulling the trigger farther, against an additional spring, gives automatic fire. But the firing mechanism can be exchanged for one giving only single shots, or one which gives single shots and three-round bursts for a single pressure on the trigger. By changing the bolt and switching the ejection port cover to one side or the other, the rifle can easily be suited to right- or left-handed firers.

Specification:
Calibre: 5·56mm NATO
Operation: Gas, selective fire
Weight: 3·60kg
Length: 790mm
Barrel: 508mm, 6 grooves, right-hand twist
Magazine: 30- or 42-round box
Rate of fire: 650 rds/min.
Muzzle velocity: 975 m/sec.

Steyr AUG is capable of being assembled in varying forms; above left shows the rifle, short rifle, carbine and short carbine variations in 5.56mm calibre. The carrying-handle/sight unit can be changed for a telescope mounting bracket, and the firing mechanism can be changed to provide various choices of single-shot, automatic or burst fire.

Manufacturer: Steyr-Mannlicher GmbH, Steyr

This was Steyr's first modern military rifle, though 'modern' in this context needs some qualifying. In the early 1960s, when armies were equipping with modern automatic rifles, many of them came to the conclusion that these weapons were not sufficiently accurate for sniping, and the usual solution was to retain some of their old bolt-action weapons for the task. The only problem with that solution was that these bolt-action weapons were, by that time, obsolescent and wearing out. Steyr-Mannlicher saw in this an opportunity to provide a new bolt action of excellent accuracy, using some modern technology.

The **SSG (Scharfschützen Gewehr) 69** was adopted by the Austrian Army in 1969, and this adoption was followed by several others. So far as the mechanical aspect went, the design was fairly conventional, using a turn-bolt action, but the bolt was a new design by Steyr which used six rear lugs to lock the bolt into the receiver. Theoretically, rear lugs are not conducive to accuracy since they allow a degree of compression of the bolt on firing, but by deeply seating the barrel into the receiver Steyr appear to have overcome this. The magazine is the Schoenauer rotary magazine which first appeared in 1887 and, in its perfected form, was used in the Greek Army Mannlicher service rifle of 1903 and in many Mannlicher-Schoenauer sporting rifles and carbines since then. The magazine is a spool which fits neatly into the stock and which can be loaded from a charger; loading the rounds winds up a spring which can then drive the spool to feed cartridges to the bolt. The entire unit can be withdrawn beneath the rifle and has a transparent rear cover which allows the contents to be checked at any time. For those who prefer, a 10-round box magazine can be substituted for the rotary one.

The stock is of plastic material; this was among the first major applications of plastic to a complete rifle stock rather than just butt and fore-end, and proved entirely serviceable; it was doubtless

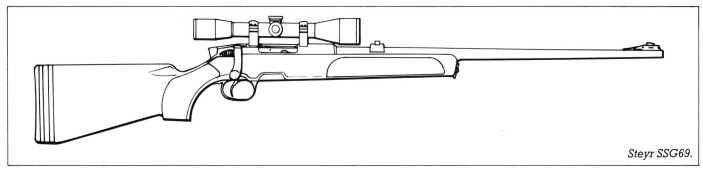

Steyr SSG69.

this experience which led to the plastic stock of the AUG.

The **SSG69** is provided with a conventional V-notch rear sight and blade foresight, but these are solely for emergency use, and the receiver is formed into a mount to which virtually any sighting telescope can be fitted. The rifle is normally supplied with a Kahles ZF69 sighting telescope of 6x magnification, graduated up to 800 metres.

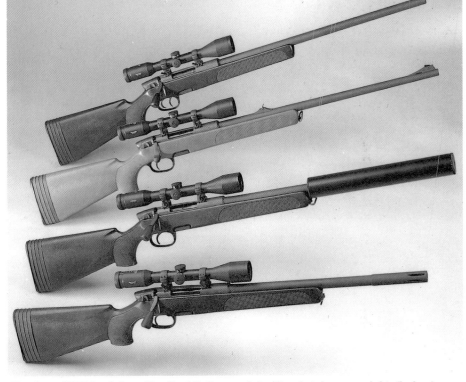

The Steyr SSG69 sniping rifle: (top) Police model with only telescope sight; (below) Standard, with iron and telescope sights; (below) Suppressed model with built-in silencer; (bottom) Special model with short barrel and flash hider.

Specification:
Calibre: 7·62mm NATO
Operation: Bolt-action repeater
Length: 1140mm
Weight, empty: 3·9kg
Barrel: 650mm, 4 grooves, right-hand twist
Magazine: 15-round rotary or 10-round box
Muzzle velocity: 860 m/sec.

**Manufacturer: Fabrique Nationale
d'Armes de Guerre, Herstal**

The FN company began developing an automatic rifle in the mid-1930s, and in 1949 produced an excellent traditional design which was adopted by several armies. However, they were also astute enough to realise that by adopting modern manufacturing methods and striking away from the traditional wooden-stocked design they could produce a sound weapon at a competitive price. In the early 1950s NATO were wrangling over their standard cartridge and FN gambled that the American proposal which eventually became the 7.62mm round would

win. They therefore developed their new rifle around this cartridge, so that when NATO settled on it and the members all looked round for a rifle, FN were ready with the **FAL (Fusil Automatique Léger)**. Since 1953, when the first customers appeared, the FAL has been adopted by over 70 armies and has been made under licence in several countries.

The FAL is gas operated and uses a tilting bolt mechanism derived from the earlier 1949 rifle. There is a bolt inside a bolt carrier, and the carrier has a shaped cam surface which acts against lugs on each side of the bolt. On firing, gas is directed into a cylinder above the barrel, where it drives a short-stroke piston

back to deliver a sharp blow to the bolt carrier. This starts moving back, and has a short free movement, allowing pressure to drop in the bore, before the cam contacts the bolt lugs and lifts the rear of the bolt up, disengaging it from a locking surface in the receiver. The bolt and carrier then run back and are returned by a spring to reload the chamber. As the bolt closes, the carrier continues forward and another cam surface forces the bolt down into its locking recess. A hammer is cocked during the rearward stroke.

As originally designed, the firing mechanism gave single shots and automatic fire, but the rifle is rather

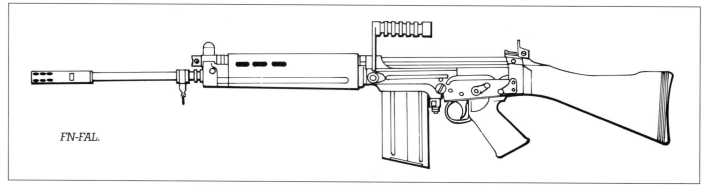

FN-FAL.

The FN-FAL rifle with short barrel and folding metal butt.

light for automatic fire and most customers opted for single-shot only mechanisms.

A heavy-barrelled **FALO (Fusil Automatique Lourd)** version with a bipod was provided for those who wanted a squad automatic weapon, but this proved to be a role for which the FAL was unsuited. For reasons that have never been satisfactorily explained, many supposedly fully automatic weapons proved to jam on the second shot. Consequently, many were restricted to semi-automatic fire and other LSW solutions were found in the shape of the Minimi and comparable 5.56mm-calibre light machine guns. However, the heavy-barrelled FAL has sometimes proved to be a useful sniping rifle.

The standard **Type 50-00** rifle has a wooden or plastic fixed butt and a 533mm barrel. There is also a folding-butt **Type 50-64** 'Para' model, with the standard barrel, and a compact **Type 50-63** 'Para' with a 436mm barrel. The **Type 50-41** FALO

The FN-FAL with standard barrel and fitted with an image-intensifying night sight.

has a special 533mm heavy barrel, and weighs 6kg empty.

A variety of flash eliminators can be found, some of which can be used for grenade launching, and bayonets have ranged from conventional knives to tube-hilt patterns doubling as flash-hiders. In general, the FN-FAL could be configured any way the customer wanted it, within limits.

In addition to the guns made in Belgium by Fabrique Nationale d'Armes de Guerre and its successors, many FALs have been made elsewhere. The British Army issued the infantry rifle as the **L1A1**, made by BSA and in the ordnance factory in Enfield Lock; rifles and light-support weapons have been made in quantity in Argentina (**FSL** rifles), Australia (British-type L1A1 rifles), Brazil (**M964** rifle, **M969A1** paratroop rifle), Canada (**C1** and **C1A1** rifles; **C2** and **C2A1** heavy rifles), India (**1-A SL** rifle) and South Africa (**R1** rifle). In addition, factories in Israel, Mexico and Venezuela assembled rifles from Belgian-made parts.

Specification (standard FAL):
Calibre: 7.62mm NATO
Operation: Gas, semi-automatic or selective fire
Length: 1053mm
Weight: 4.31kg
Barrel: 533mm, 4 grooves, right-hand twist
Magazine: 20-round box
Rate of fire: 650 rds/min
Muzzle velocity: 853 m/sec

Left: A typical heavy-barrel FALO, showing its bipod.

Right: An exploded-view drawing of the FAL.

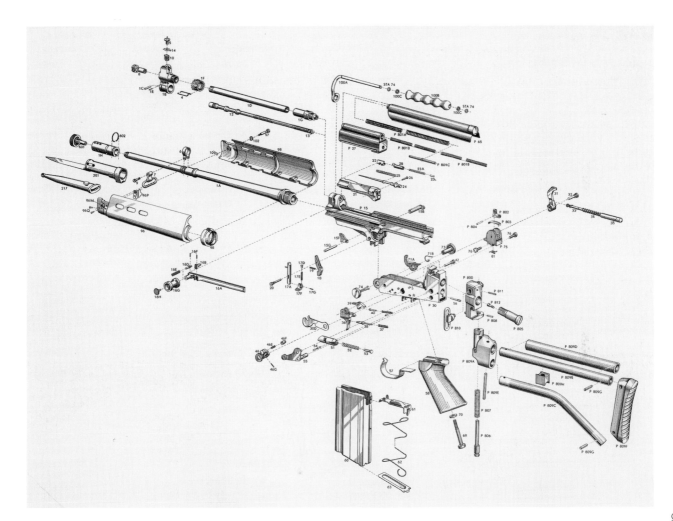

95

FN-FNC

Belgium

Manufacturer: FN Herstal SA, Herstal

FN were quick to realise the importance of the 7·62mm NATO cartridge and had a rifle ready for the demand; in the early 1970s they tried to repeat this with a 5·56mm rifle, the CAL, which was more or less a scaled-down FAL model. This, however, appeared at the wrong time, when most armies still had considerable mileage left in their 7·62mm weapons and were not ready to make the change of calibre until everybody else was of the same mind. As a result the CAL rifle failed to find a market; moreover, it was soon found to be too expensive and insufficiently reliable. FN therefore developed an entirely new 5·56mm assault rifle and entered it into the 1977 NATO trials, but this, too, was premature and the weapon was withdrawn for further development.

In 1982 the new rifle, the **FN-FNC**, eventually appeared. It was a gas-operated weapon but instead of the FAL's tilting bolt or the multiple-thread bolt of the CAL, the **FNC** uses a simple two-lug rotating bolt similar in general principle to that of the M16. A gas piston above the barrel drives back the bolt carrier; inside this is the bolt, the rotation of which is driven by a lug propelled by a cam track in the carrier. A return spring is compressed and the hammer cocked during the recoil stroke, and the return stroke loads a fresh round into the chamber and rotates the bolt to lock it. The gas regulator is simply an on-off tap, on for normal fire and off for launching grenades. The gas system is self-regulating; whatever amount of gas is required to start the bolt moving is taken, and once the piston moves back it releases any further gas to atmosphere.

Light alloys, pressed steel and plastics are used in the construction, resulting in a commendably light rifle. The firing mechanism offers single shots, three-round bursts or automatic fire. The barrel can be obtained rifled to suit either the original US M193 bullet or

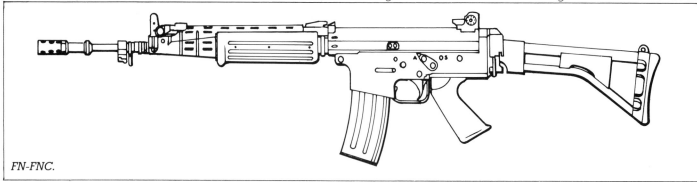

FN-FNC.

the NATO-standardised Belgian SS109 bullet.

The **FNC** is made in two versions; the first is the standard rifle with full length barrel and either a plastic fixed butt or a tubular metal folding butt. The second is a carbine version with a short (363mm) barrel with the same butt options. In addition there is also a **'Law Enforcement'** version of the standard rifle which has a firing mechanism capable only of single shot semi-automatic fire. The **FNC** is in service with the Belgian Army, is made under licence in Indonesia and, in somewhat modified form, is the Swedish Army standard rifle.

The upper picture shows that the FNC is a relatively simple weapon to strip and maintain, while the lower picture shows that it can be used left-handed as well.

Specification (Standard rifle):
Calibre: 5·56mm
Operation: Gas, selective fire
Length (butt extended): 997mm (butt fixed; 766mm (butt folded)
Weight: 3·8kg
Barrel: 449mm, 6 grooves, right-hand twist
Magazine: 30-round box
Rate of fire: 600-750 rds/min.
Muzzle velocity: 965 m/sec.

ČZ58   Czechoslovakia

Manufacturer: Česzkoslovenska
Zbrojowka, Uhersky Brod
(Variant Models: 58P, 58V, 58Pi)

The standard rifle of almost all Warsaw Pact and Communist-backed countries was the Kalashnikov AK, with the exception of the armed forces of Czechoslovakia. The Czechs had an extremely good indigenous arms industry by 1939, and they were prompt to get it back into operating order after 1945. As a result they had some excellent weapon designs available, and instead of accepting the Kalashnikov they opted for their own

rifle. The ČZ58 does tend to resemble an AK and fools many people, but it is a totally different weapon.

The weapon is gas operated, with a cylinder mounted above the barrel; there is no gas regulator, the full force of the gas being delivered to the piston, but there are vents in the cylinder which, once the piston has been given sufficient momentum and moved past the vents, allows the surplus gas to escape. The piston makes a short stroke, striking a bolt carrier and driving it rearward. The bolt, inside the carrier, is rectangular

and a hinged locking piece is engaged in front of the shoulders in the receiver. The carrier moves back some 22mm, giving ample time for the chamber pressure to drop, and then inclined planes in the carrier lift the locking piece free from the locking shoulders and then carry the bolt to the rear, extracting the empty case, cocking the hammer and compressing a return spring.

On the return stroke the bolt face collects a cartridge from the magazine and loads it into the chamber. The bolt closes up behind the case, and the

ČZ58.V

98

carrier, moving forward, drives the locking piece down into the engagement with the shoulders on the receiver, so locking the bolt firmly. On pressing the trigger the hammer strikes a firing pin in the bolt and the cartridge is fired.

The standard model is the **ČZ58P**, with a solid butt; early models used wood but since the early 1960s the butt has been of wood-impregnated plastic material. The **ČZ58V** is the same rifle but with a folding single-strut metal butt which folds sideways to lie alongside the receiver. The **ČZ58Pi** is the standard P model but with a special bracket attached to the right side for mounting a night vision sight. This version usually has a large flash-hider attached to the muzzle and a light bipod.

Specification:
Calibre: 7·62mm Czech M45 or 7·62mm Soviet M43
Operation: Gas, selective fire
Length: 843mm
Weight: 3·11kg
Barrel: 400mm, 4 grooves, right-hand twist
Magazine: 30-round box
Rate of fire: 800 rds/min.
Muzzle velocity: 710 m/sec.

Though it may resemble the Kalashnikov, the Czech service rifle is an entirely different weapon.

SAKO M/62 Assault Rifle Series　Finland

Manufacturers Oy Sako and Sako-Valmet (Variants: M/62, M62/76, M/95)

The Finnish Army, seeking to replace its ageing bolt-action Mosin-Nagants, elected to adapt a Kalashnikov derivative in the mid-1950s. Several prototypes led to the semi-experimental **M/60**, one pattern being developed by Valmet and another by Sako. The best features of the two rivals were then combined in the **M/62**. The receiver was simplified, the ribbed plastic hand guard varied, and the pistol grip took different forms.

The action was a straightforward copy of the Kalashnikov (*q.v.*), though the gas tube of the original guns generally lay in a stamped liner, with the top exposed. The back sight attachment was improved in the late 1960s, when a solid front-sight hood replaced the original open pattern. Selectors were marked • (single shots) and ••• (automatic fire).

From 1972 onward, tritium night sights were fitted to new guns and the rounded back sight protectors were replaced by taller square versions. Rifles with the original sights were then reclassified as **M/62 TP**. Production of the folding-butt M/62 TP recommenced in 1985, as the machined-steel receiver had proved to be more durable than its M/76 successor.

Introduced in 1977, the **M/76** (or 'M/62/76') had a sheet-steel receiver. Though this did not prove to be durable enough to impress the Finnish Army, M/76 rifles were sold in quantity to Qatar and Indonesia and have provided the basis for a variety of commercial selective-fire derivatives.

On 1 January 1987, Sako and Valmet amalgamated as 'Sako-Valmet Oy'. Work on an improved assault rifle recommenced, with 'M/90' prototypes appearing in 1989–90. The selector was moved to the left side of the receiver, a spring-loaded cover plate was added to prevent snow and dust entering the charging-handle slot, and other improvements were made internally. However, the army decided that interchangeability was paramount and so the simpler 'M/92/62' became the **M/95 TP**.

This has a tubular butt that can swing forward alongside the receiver; a rail for optical and electro-optical sights on the left side of the receiver; a 'cranked' charging handle that can be retracted with the left hand; tritium 'dusk sights'; and an improved brake/compensator. Unfortunately, a decision was taken to end assault-rifle production in Finland in 1997 and the future of the distinctive Finnish Kalashnikov derivatives remains uncertain.

Specification (M/90 prototype):
Calibre: 7.62mm Soviet M43
Operation: Gas, selective fire
Length: 930mm with butt extended
Weight: 3.85kg without magazine
Barrel: 416mm, 4 grooves, right-hand twist
Magazine: 30-round box
Rate of fire: 600–750 rds/min
Muzzle velocity: 710 m/sec

Above right: A typical Valmet-made M62/76 rifle.

Right: The abortive Sako-Valmet M/90 assault rifle.

SAKO TRG-21 SNIPER'S RIFLE   Finland

Manufacturer: Sako Ltd, Riihimäki

This rifle was introduced in 1989 and represents the most recent thinking in the design of sniping rifles from a company long known for precision weapons.

The **TRG-21** consists of a heavy stainless steel barrel screwed into a tubular receiver. The receiver is, unusually, cold-hammered from steel in the same manner as the barrel, instead of, as is more usual, being machined from the solid. This should give excellent strength for the minimum weight and,

due to work-hardening under the hammers, exceptional resistance to wear. The receiver and barrel are attached to an aluminium sub-frame by three screws, so making a completely rigid structure, yet allowing the barrel to float freely. There is a small but efficient muzzle brake at the end of the barrel; it is probable that this can be removed and replaced by a silencer.

The bolt is of conventional type, with three front lugs and a fourth formed by the handle turning down into a recess. The opening movement is a 60° lift.

The trigger mechanism, of high-grade steel, is fully adjustable as to the position of the trigger, so as to suit the firer's hand, and the first-stage travel (first pressure) and weight of pull are also adjustable. A detachable magazine, also of high-grade steel, is concealed inside the stock. There is a silent-operating safety catch on the right side of the receiver, and at the rear of the bolt is an indicator showing whether or not the rifle is cocked.

The stock is made from injection-moulded polyurethane and encloses

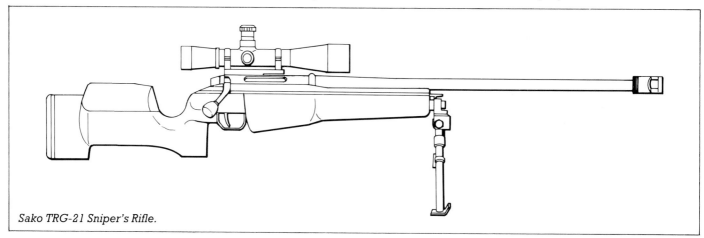

Sako TRG-21 Sniper's Rifle.

the aluminium sub-frame. The butt is formed into a pistol grip and has a series of distance and angle plates provided which allow the user to adjust the length and the height of the cheek-piece to suit his own stature. At the front of the sub-frame an adjustable steel bipod is fitted.

Conventional iron sights are not fitted; there is a 17mm dovetail sight mount formed into the receiver, on to which any preferred optical or electro-optical sight can be fitted. The mount also includes a set of fold-down emergency sights.

As with all sniping rifles the success of this weapon depends largely upon the ammunition, and Sako recommend the use of their own ·308 Winchester special cartridges which are carefully manufactured for precision shooting.

Specification:
Cartridge: 7·62mm NATO
(·308 Winchester)
Operation: Manual, single-shot
Length: 1150mm
Weight: 4·7kg without sights
Barrel: 660mm, 4 grooves, right-hand twist
Magazine: 10-round double-row box
Muzzle velocity: 840 m/sec.

The TRG rifles are now available in two calibres; the TRG21 (below) in 7.62mm NATO and the TRG41, similar but chambered for the exceptionally accurate .338 Lapua Magnum cartridge.

FUSIL AUTOMATIQUE MAS (FA-MAS) France

Manufacturer: Manufacture d'Armes de St Etienne

The French Army was the first European army to adopt the 5.56mm cartridge as their standard infantry calibre, when they introduced the **FA-MAS (Fusil Automatique, Manufacture d'Armes de Saint Etienne)** in 1980. Since then it has been sold to a number of ex-French colonies including Djibouti and Gabon, and to Lebanon and the United Arab Emirates.

The FA-MAS is a bullpup rifle, with the action set well back into the stock so as to give maximum barrel length in a compact weapon. The action is delayed blowback, using a two-part bolt of unusual design. The bolt is carried in a heavy bolt carrier and the two are connected by a curved lever; as the bolt closes, the carrier continues forward and rotates the lever forward so that it engages in front of a lug in the floor of the receiver. On firing, the pressure in the chamber forces the cartridge

case back against the bolt; this presses back against the lever and attempts to rotate it backwards so as to lift the toe from the lug. But the top of the lever bears against the heavy bolt carrier, and the leverage ratio means that there is quite a strong resistance to the initial movement. This is sufficient to allow the bullet to leave the barrel and the chamber pressure to drop. Eventually the bolt pressure turns the lever and thrusts the carrier back, lifts the lever toe free and the whole assembly begins

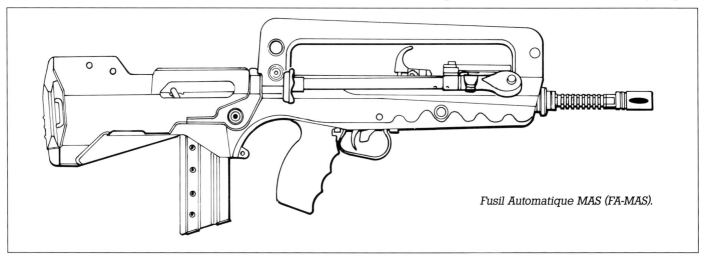

Fusil Automatique MAS (FA-MAS).

to run backwards to reload and re-cock the weapon. The lever is also interlinked to the firing pin and firing mechanism so that the rifle cannot fire until the lever has rotated into the locked position.

The system works satisfactorily, but is rather marginal – most cartridge cases show signs of bulging, indicating that the bolt has started to move backwards and extract the case before the pressure has reached a really safe figure. As with most blowback weapons using bottle-necked cases, the interior of the chamber is grooved to allow propellant gas to pass down outside the cartridge case and equalise the pressure inside and out, thus preventing the case sticking.

Several variant models have been shown at exhibitions in the past decade. These include an export model without automatic fire, a short-barrel 'Commando' model, and a civilian model chambered for the .222 Remington cartridge and capable only of single shot firing.

The **FA-MAS G2**, adopted by the French forces in 1995, is instantly identifiable by the elongated trigger guard and by the shaping of the fore-end to prevent the firer's hand slipping forward in front of the muzzle. The original guns were retrospectively re-classified **G1**.

Specification:
Calibre: 5.56mm NATO
Operation: Delayed blowback, selective fire, with burst firing capability
Length: 757mm
Weight: 3.61 kg

Barrel: 488mm, 3 grooves, right-hand twist
Magazine: 25-round box
Rate of fire: 900–1000 rds/min
Muzzle velocity: 960 m/sec

French soldiers call the FA-MAS rifle 'le clairon' (the bugle) from the shape of the carrying handle.

SNIPING RIFLE FR-F1   France

**Manufacturer: Manufacture
d'Armes de St. Etienne
(Variant Model: FR-F2)**

Traditionally, and like most armies, the French used selected specimens of their standard service rifle as sniping weapons, fitting them with telescope sights. The adoption of the 5·56mm FA-MAS rifle ended this, and it became necessary to develop a specialised sniping rifle. And, also like other armies, the French Army fell back upon its last bolt action weapon, the

MAS Modèle 1936 for the basic mechanism, adapted it into a modern weapon, and called the result the **Fusil à Répétition F1.**

The MAS 36 bolt action uses an unusually large diameter bolt which is in one piece. The two locking lugs are at the rear end and lock into recesses in the side walls of the receiver close to the bridge. The mainspring is inside the hollow firing pin, rather than wrapped around it as is the more usual practice. The bolt handle is turned

down, and differs considerably from the MAS 36 pattern which was bent forward to place it close to the firer's hand to allow rapid fire; this is less necessary on a sniping rifle.

A pistol grip is fitted, and the stock, as with the MAS 36, is in two pieces, fore-end and butt, which are bolted to the deep receiver. A ten-round box magazine is inserted from below, and the bottom of the magazine carries a large rubber pad; when the magazine is removed, this pad can be taken from

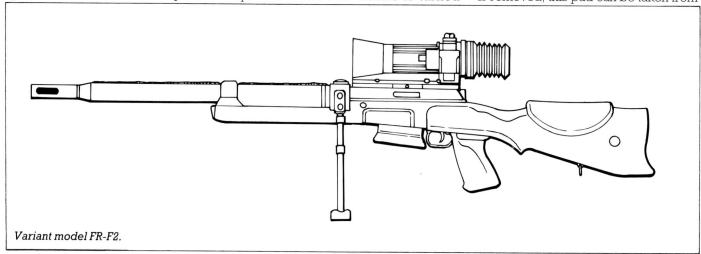

Variant model FR-F2.

106

the bottom and slipped over the mouth of the magazine to keep out dust and dirt. A bipod is fixed at the rear of the fore-end, and this, together with a muzzle brake, gives the rifle excellent steadiness and a quick return to the aim after firing.

Unlike many sniping rifles, a good set of iron sights, complete with luminous spots for firing in poor light, is fitted, but the primary sight is, of course, a telescope which is issued with the rifle and carried in its own case.

The **FR-F1** was originally issued in 7·5mm French Service calibre, but was later made in 7·62mm NATO chambering.

In 1984 the **FR-F2** rifle was issued; this is much the same but with improvements; the bipod has been strengthened, and slightly moved, to a position where it is less likely to affect barrel vibration, and the fore-end is now of plastic-coated steel. Most novel is the enclosure of the barrel in a thermal insulating sleeve, designed to prevent the barrel bending in strong sunlight, reduce the thermal air disturbance in the sight line and also reduce the infrared signature of the weapon.

Specification:
Calibre: 7·5mm French or 7·62m NATO
Operation: Manual, single-shot
Weight: 5·20kg
Length: 1138mm
Barrel: 552mm
Magazine: 10-round box
Muzzle velocity: 852 m/sec. (7·62mm)

The FR-F1 (below) and F2 (left) are based upon an elderly bolt action but both are extremely accurate sniping rifles.

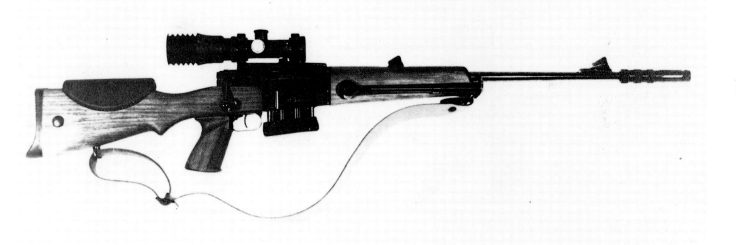

Manufacturer: Heckler & Koch GmbH, Oberndorf-am-Neckar

In 1945, despite Germany's imminent defeat, the Mauser factory in Oberndorf was developing a new assault rifle using a roller-locked delayed-blowback breech mechanism. The war ended before the design was perfected, the designers left and settled in Spain, and the rifle development was taken up by CETME. They licensed it to a Dutch company, Nederlandsch Wapen en Munitiefabriek, who interested the newly re-formed German Army in the design. But the army were not satisfied with it and passed it to Heckler & Koch to be reworked and brought to perfection. NWM relinquished their licence and Heckler & Koch developed the design into the Gewehr 3, which was adopted by the Bundeswehr and has since been widely adopted around the world, being made under licence in several countries. It is probably the most widely-distributed rifle in the Western world after the FN-FAL.

The G3 breech block is in two pieces; as it closes the heavier rear portion forces out two rollers into recesses in the receiver, so locking the breech. On firing, the light head is forced back by the cartridge case but has to drive the rollers out of their recesses, in turn forcing the heavy bolt body backwards. This is a slow process, slow enough to allow the bullet to leave the barrel and the bore pressure to drop before the breech begins to open. The bolt then goes back, a hammer is cocked, and in the return stroke the rifle is re-loaded.

The G3 has one or two innovative features; it was the first to mount the

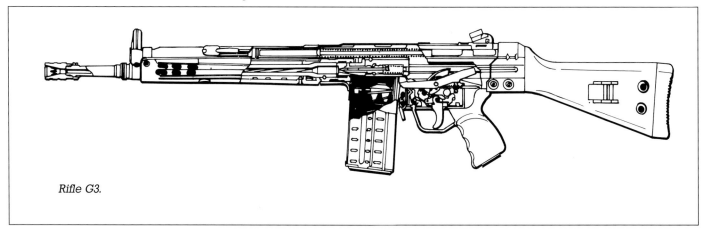

Rifle G3.

cocking handle well forward on the upper side of the fore-end, so that reaching it is a very easy and natural movement. An extension on the bolt runs forward into the cocking-handle tube and helps to balance the action of the bolt. Twelve longitudinal grooves are cut into the front of the chamber, allowing propellant gas to seep down the outside of the case to balance the internal pressure and prevent the case sticking too tightly in the chamber (a defect otherwise common in blowback-operated weapons).

The basic **G3** has a wooden butt and simple two-position rear sight; the **G3A1** has a telescoping butt; the **G3A2** was a G3 with a drum-type adjustable rear sight which has since become standard on all models; the **G3A3** has a plastic butt and fore-end and is the current model; the **G3A4** has a telescoping stock The **G3A3 Zf** is fitted as standard with a telescope sight, and the **G3/SG 1** is a selected G3A3 with a zoom telescope sight, bipod and precision trigger assembly which is capable of being set to hair-trigger and adjusted for pull-off. Rifles have also been made in Denmark (**G3A5**), Iran (**G3A6**) and Pakistan (**G3A7**). These can be identified by their markings, which,

in the case of the Pakistani guns, may be in Arabic script. Otherwise-standard G3A3 guns made in Greece display a mark in the form of an encircled 'EBO' monogram.

Below: Two standard-barrel versions of the G3 rifle, one with collapsible butt and the other with the fixed plastic butt.

Specification (G3A3):
Calibre: 7.62mm NATO
Length: 1025mm
Weight: 4.40kg
Barrel: 450mm, 4 grooves, right-hand twist
Magazine: 20-round box
Rate of fire: 500–600 rds/min
Muzzle velocity: 790 m/sec

RIFLE G41   Germany

Manufacturer: Heckler & Koch GmbH, Oberndorf-am-Neckar

Heckler & Koch followed up the G3 rifle with the HK33, a 5·56mm weapon which appeared in the early 1970s. Like the contemporary FN-CAL it was somewhat ahead of its time, since most major armies were waiting to see what the American experience with 5·56mm was before they committed themselves, but the HK33 made some useful overseas sales and showed that H&K were on the right lines. It was essentially a scaled-down G3 rifle, using exactly the same bolt system and laid out in the same manner.

In the late 1970s the three-round burst idea was becoming popular; at the same time, H&K were working on their caseless G11 rifle, and they doubtless felt that it might be a good idea to develop a new 5·56mm weapon with a three-round burst capability which would be available for export and, if the G11 should fail, might be a fall-back for German Army adoption. Whatever the reasoning behind it, the **G41** was developed, and this has proved to be a most impressive rifle.

In essence, once more it is the familiar H&K roller-locked delayed blowback breech system used in the G3 and scaled down to suit the 5·56mm cartridge. The firing mechanism has been redesigned to allow single shots, three-round bursts, or full automatic fire, and the barrel is rifled with a twist of one turn in 178mm so as to suit the new NATO standard 5·56mm bullet. In addition, NATO standardisation has been carried a good deal further; the magazine housing is to NATO

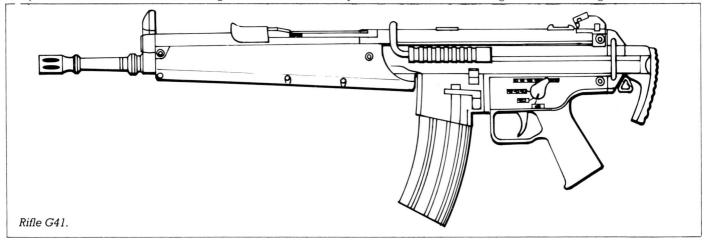

Rifle G41.

Standardisation Agreement (STANAG) 4179 which is based upon the dimensions of the M16 magazine, and thus the **G41** will accept M16 and any other NATO standardised magazine – for example, that of the British L85 rifle. There is also a sight mount to NATO STANAG 2324 which means that any standardised telescope sight or night vision sight will fit on to the **G41**. Other features include a positive bolt closure which is completely silent in operation, a new bolt catch to keep the bolt to the rear after the magazine has been emptied, a mounting for a bipod and a dust cover on the case ejection port.

As with the G3, the **G41** is available with a fixed plastic butt or a telescoping butt, with a long barrel or short barrel. A small number have been purchased by the Bundeswehr; it was originally suggested that when the G11 rifle became standard issue, non-infantry units would be armed with the **G41**, but with the collapse of the G11 it seems unlikely that the **G41** will enter German service in any quantity.

Specification:
Calibre: 5·56mm NATO
Operation: Delayed blowback, selective fire
Length: 997mm (butt fixed); 806mm (butt folded)
Weight: 4·35kg
Barrel: 450mm, 6 grooves, right-hand twist
Magazine: 30-round box
Rate of fire: 850 rds/min.
Muzzle velocity: 935 m/sec.

The H&K G41 rifle with fixed butt. Note the fire selector, giving Safe, Single, Three-round and Automatic positions.

RIFLE G8 Germany

Manufacturer: Heckler & Koch GmbH, Oberndorf-am-Neckar

Following the successful development of their G3 and other rifles, Heckler & Koch applied the same basic delayed-blowback bolt mechanism to a number of light machine gun designs in both 7·62mm and 5·56mm calibres. One of these was the HK11 7·62mm machine gun, which evolved into the HK11E, and this latter design was notable for the fact that it could easily be converted from magazine to belt feed or vice versa. In the early 1980s, in response to various suggestions from

European police forces, they redeveloped the HK11E and turned it into the **G8** rifle, a weapon which is one of the most versatile ever manufactured.

The object in view was to develop a weapon which would give a police squad whatever type of firepower they needed to deal with a given situation, without their having to carry a complete armoury around with them. In this one weapon there is every type of response that could possibly be required.

In basic form it is a standard Heckler & Koch delayed blowback rifle, using the

familiar roller-locked bolt. It is, though, provided with single shot, three-round burst and automatic fire options, and the barrel is much heavier than usual and precision rifled so that it can act as a perfectly adequate sniping rifle. For this purpose it is fitted not only with standard iron sights but also has a telescope mount which is to NATO standards and will accept any telescope sight or night vision sight.

Where more firepower is required, the standard box magazine can be replaced with a special 50-round drum magazine. Should this not be sufficient,

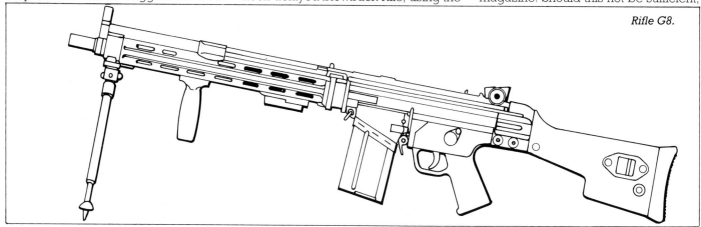

Rifle G8.

112

then the entire magazine housing can be quickly removed and replaced by a belt feed unit. The bolt is also removed and replaced by a different bolt assembly, and the weapon then becomes a belt-fed machine gun. Since this type of weapon is generally used to produce sustained fire, the barrel of the **G8** can be quickly removed and replaced with a fresh barrel when it gets too hot.

For those forces who do not see a requirement for the automatic fire option, the **G8A1** variant is capable only of single shot fire, but retains the quick-change heavy barrel and telescope sight mounting.

The **G8** has been adopted by the West German Border Police and several other state police forces as armament for their anti-terrorist squads.

Specification:

Calibre: 7·62mm NATO
Operation (G8): Delayed blowback, selective fire
Weight: 8·15kg with bipod
Length: 1030mm
Barrel: 450mm, 6 grooves, right-hand twist
Magazine: 20-round box, 50-round drum or belt
Rate of fire: 800 rds/min.
Muzzle velocity: 835 m/sec.

The G8 rifle is perhaps the most versatile rifle ever made.

MAUSER SP66   Germany

Manufacturer: Mauser-Werke Oberndorf GmbH, Oberndorf-am-Neckar

The German Army do not tie themselves to one specific weapon in each class, but spread their purchasing around between various makers so as to maintain a sound manufacturing base. As a result, in addition to the Heckler & Koch rifles in the sniping role, they also deploy a large number of **Mauser SP66** rifles.

The **Mauser SP66** is actually based upon a commercial sporting rifle the 'Model SP66S Super Match', though various modifications have been made to suit it to employment by military and police agencies. It is a bolt action rifle using Mauser's 'short action' bolt mechanism; in this design, the bolt handle is actually fitted to the forward end of the bolt, just behind the locking lugs. In point of fact the opening stroke of the bolt is no shorter than any other, since it must move back a finite distance to allow the cartridge to enter the boltway, but the placement of the bolt handle means a much shorter movement of the firer's hand and a quicker return to the trigger after reloading. It does mean that the action body can be some 90mm shorter, and instead of merely using this to shorten the rifle, the saved amount has been added to the barrel length. The barrel is fitted with a very efficient muzzle brake and flash eliminator, specially developed to completely do away with flash, since this rifle is intended to be used with high-power telescope or night vision sights which can easily be blinded by excessive flash.

The wooden stock is of the thumb-hole pattern giving an excellent grip for the firing hand, and the length of butt and height of cheek-piece can be adjusted to suit the firer. All wooden surfaces in contact with the hand have been roughened, the fore-end is wider than usual, and the trigger has a wide shoe so that the hands have a firm grip and control of the weapon.

There are no iron sights fitted; the receiver is formed into a telescope

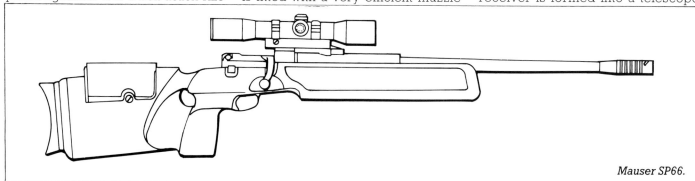

Mauser SP66.

114

mount and the rifle is supplied as standard with a Zeiss Diavari ZA 1·5x-6x zoom telescope sight. A special adapter to fit on the telescope mount and adapt it to night vision image intensifying sights is also provided.

Two views of the Mauser SP66 fitted with an image-intensifying night sight. It is now available with a specially-fitted silencer in place of the muzzle brake.

Specification:
Calibre: 7·62mm NATO
Operation: Manual, single-shot
Length: Approx. 1200mm depending upon butt adjustment
Weight, empty: 6·12kg with Zeiss telescope
Barrel: 650mm, 6 grooves, right-hand twist
Magazine: 3-round integral box
Muzzle velocity: 868 m/sec.

RIFLE G36   Germany

*Manufacturer: Heckler & Koch
GmbH, Oberndorf-am-Neckar
(Variant models: G36E, G36K,
MG36, MG36E)*

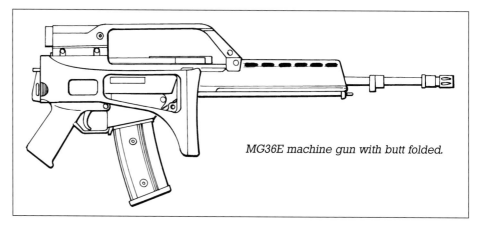

MG36E machine gun with butt folded.

When the **G11** programme was
cancelled the German Army was left
without a 5.56mm rifle to conform to
NATO standard. It had been intended
to issue second-line units with the
G41 rifle when first-line troops
received the G11, but it seems that
this would have been too expensive
in the post-Cold War financial
climate. The German Army therefore
undertook a very rapid comparative
trial between a new Heckler & Koch
design and the existing **Steyr AUG**,
with the result that the H&K design
was selected and became the
Gewehr 36. (Note that this design
has no connection whatever with an
earlier experimental G36 which H&K
designed around a 4.6mm bullet in
the 1970s.)

The G36 broke new ground as far
as H&K were concerned; for the first
time (apart from the G11) they
abandoned their well-tried roller-
locked delayed blowback system
and, in the interests of cheapness
and simplicity, went for a gas-
operated rotating bolt solution. It also
reduced the weight and allowed
for widely-differing ammunition
characteristics. Apart from a rather
slab-sided appearance, the layout is
conventional, with the gas cylinder
beneath the barrel, a pistol grip, box
magazine, and folding tubular butt. A
raised sight block at the rear of the
receiver carries a 3x optical sight,
and the integral carrying handle runs
from this block to the front end of the
receiver, with an aperture in the
forward end to permit the line of
sight to pass through. The cocking
handle is underneath the carrying
handle and also acts as a bolt-
closing assist if needed.

The G36 was adopted by the
German Army in 1996. An export
version, the **G36E**, is also available;
this differs only in the optical sight,
the G36E having a 1.5x telescope. A
short-barrelled version, the **G36K**, is
issued to German special forces; it
differs in having a prong-type flash
hider.

Specification (G36):
Calibre: 5.56x45mm NATO
Operation: Gas-operated, rotating bolt
Length: 998mm butt extended; 758mm butt folded
Weight, empty: 3.43kg
Barrel: 480mm, 6 grooves, right-hand twist
Magazine: 30-round detachable box
Cyclic rate: 750 rds/min
Muzzle velocity: approx. 920 m/sec

Specification (G36K):
Calibre: 5.56x45mm NATO
Operation: Gas-operated, rotating bolt
Length: 858mm butt extended; 613mm butt folded
Weight, empty: 3.13kg
Barrel: 320mm, 6 grooves, right-hand twist
Magazine: 30-round detachable box
Cyclic rate: 750 rds/min
Muzzle velocity: approx. 850 m/sec

HK MG36

This is a variant of the **G36** rifle, intended to be used as the squad automatic weapon. This is something of a surprise since the German Army was the originator of, and has remained the principal supporter of, the general-purpose machine gun, but the change in rifle calibres has eventually led them to a change in machine-gun tactics. The **MG36** has a somewhat heavier barrel, and is fitted with a bipod, but apart from these features it is precisely the same as the rifle. A variant model, the **MG36E**, is also offered for export; like the rifles, it differs from the German service MG36 only in the optical sight, which is of 1.5x magnification instead of 3x.

Specification: MG36
Calibre: 5.56x45mm NATO
Operation: Gas-operated, rotating bolt
Length overall: 998mm
Weight, empty: 3.58kg
Barrel: 480mm, 6 grooves, right-hand twist
Magazine: 30-round detachable box
Cyclic rate: 750 rds/min
Muzzle velocity: approx. 920 m/sec

The export version, known as the G36E, differs in having a 1.5x optical sight and no red-dot sight.

NEGEV

Israel

Manufacturer: Israeli Military Industries, Ramat ha-Sharon

Though designed primarily as a light machine gun, the **Negev** represents the class of support weapon that can double as assault rifles when required, thanks to the availability of short barrels and selectable belt/box feed. Though primarily intended to feed from its own box magazines, the Negev can accept drum magazines and feed belts. Standard Galil or M16 box patterns can be used if a suitable adapter is available.

The action embodies a split piston rod and twin return springs to minimise its length, and can be dismantled into six major components without tools. Stampings and pressings have been used extensively to minimise production, but its light-machine-gun origins make the Negev a sturdy and unusually controllable (if somewhat heavy) assault rifle.

The rotating-bolt locking system was clearly inspired by the FN-Minimi, and the barrel can be rifled for either NATO or US-standard ammunition, with one turn in 178mm and 305mm respectively. The Negev fires from an open bolt, which may compromise long-range accuracy, and an adjustable gas-port, and cyclic rate varies with the gas-port setting.

The **Negev Commando** has a folding butt (only 650mm long with the butt folded) and an integral mount on the receiver for optical,

electro-optical or thermal-imaging sights. The front sight is an open post, adjustable for windage and elevation; the tangent-type aperture back sight can be adjusted from 300m to 1200m; and a folding tritium night sight is fitted.

The selector gives automatic fire or single shots, and the 'safe' position can be engaged even if the gun is cocked. Applying the safety catch automatically disconnects the trigger from the sear.

In common with guns such as the Heckler & Koch G8/HK21 (*q.v.*), which made a passable sniping rifle in addition to a satisfactory light machine gun, the Negev and the Negev Commando are finding increasing favour with Special Forces. This is partly due to the ease with which a variety of weapons can be produced from a series of standardised parts, a goal that has always been sought by the promoters of 'Weapons Systems' such as the Stoner 63 series.

Specification (Negev Commando):
Calibre: 5.56mm (.223)
Operation: Gas operated, selective fire only
Length: 820mm (butt extended)
Weight: 5.5kg
Barrel: 330mm, 6 grooves, right-hand twist.
Rate of fire, selectable: 750 and 875 rds/min

Above: The Negev, though it makes an acceptable rifle and can be fired from the shoulder eaily enough, was conceived as a light support weapon. Consequently, it is a little heavy by current assault-rifle standards.

Left: The Negev Commando, showing its compact dimensions to good advantage.

GALIL RIFLE　　　　　　　　　　　Israel

**Manufacturer: Israeli Military
Industries, Ramat ha-Sharon**

The Israeli Defence Force adopted the
7·62mm FN-FAL in the early 1950s, but
experience in their various wars with
Arab nations convinced them that
something lighter and more handy was
necessary. After the 1967 Arab-Israeli
war, the IDF asked for a new rifle, and
the **Galil** was the result, appearing in
1973.
The designer spent some time in
studying and testing every available

rifle, and soon came to the conclusion
that the reliability of the Soviet AK rifle,
which was in extensive Arab use, was
of vital importance in a desert environ-
ment. He therefore took the AK as his
model but then designed out various
points which were generally thought to
be defects and added a few things
which combat experience had suggested might be worthwhile. The
calibre of 5·56mm was selected,
though in later years, and principally
for export sales, the rifle has also been

made in 7·62mm calibre.
The AK is generally thought to have
two prime defects; it is inaccurate and
the fire selection lever is clumsy and
noisy in operation. The **Galil** cured
both these; by adopting 5·56mm but
generally retaining the bulk of the AK,
the result was rather heavy for the
calibre which gave the weapon
strength and also resisted the recoil
force and thus improved accuracy.
The fire selector was changed into a
small thumb-operated switch above

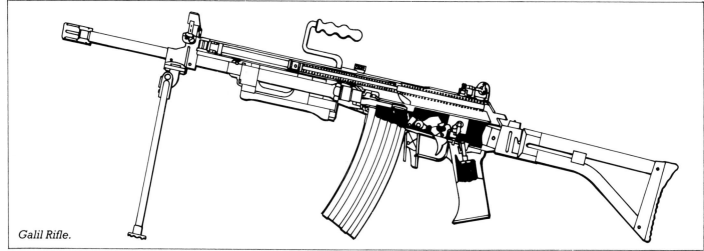

Galil Rifle.

the pistol grip on both sides of the rifle so that it is easily operated by right- or left-handed shooters. The operating system is the same top-mounted gas piston, bolt carrier and rotating bolt, and the hammer firing mechanism is also broadly similar to that of the AK. A bipod is fitted, which also acts as a wire-cutter and a bottle-opener, two examples of combat-oriented additions due to practical experience. The sights are provided with fold-up auxiliary leaves which carry luminous spots for firing in poor light, and they are generally agreed to be probably the best of their kind.

The standard rifle is known as the **ARM** and has a bipod, carrying handle and folding butt. The **Model AR** is similar but does not have the bipod or carrying handle. The **Model SAR** has a shorter (332mm) barrel, folding butt, no bipod and no carrying handle.

The **Galil** has been sold to other countries, and has also been copied in slightly modified form by the South African Defence Force who adopted it as the **R-4 rifle**, later developing a short-barrelled carbine version known as the **R-5**.

Specification (Model ARM):

Calibre: 5·56mm
Operation: Gas, selective fire
Length: 979mm (butt fixed),
742mm (butt folded)
Weight: 4·35kg
Barrel: 460mm, 6 grooves, right-hand twist
Magazine: 35-round box

Rate of fire: 650 rds/min.
Muzzle velocity: 950 m/sec.

The Galil has elements of Kalashnikov's design in it, but is far more versatile, capable of launching grenades or functioning as the squad light machine gun when fitted with an extra-capacity magazine.

GALIL SNIPER'S RIFLE   # Israel

**Manufacturer: Israeli Military
Industries, Ramat ha-Sharon**

As noted above, in discussing the 5·56mm Galil assault rifle, the design was also made somewhat larger in 7·62mm, principally for export. In the late 1970s, however, the Israel Defence Force expressed a requirement for a new sniping rifle to replace the elderly Mauser bolt-action weapons they were using in this role, and asked Israel Military Industries, makers of the Galil, to develop a suitable weapon. They took the 7·62mm Galil as their starting point

and, in close co-operation with the IDF, turned it into a highly specialised sniping weapon.

The basic mechanism is the same Kalashnikov-derived rotating bolt, operated by a gas piston and bolt carrier, as is used in the smaller Galil, merely enlarged and strengthened to deal with the heavier cartridge. The barrel is much heavier than would be used on an ordinary service rifle, giving stiffness and exceptional accuracy. The fore-end is fitted so that it does not interfere with the natural vibration of the barrel, and the

adjustable bipod is assembled to the fore-end so as not to place any strain on the rifle itself. Moreover, the bipod is set well back so that it is possible for the sniper to reach out and adjust it without having to expose himself or shift the rifle.

The muzzle is threaded and fitted with a very efficient muzzle brake and flash eliminator which assists concealment and prevents the rifle moving too far from the aim on firing. It can be unscrewed and replaced with a silencer if required.

There is, of course, no automatic fire

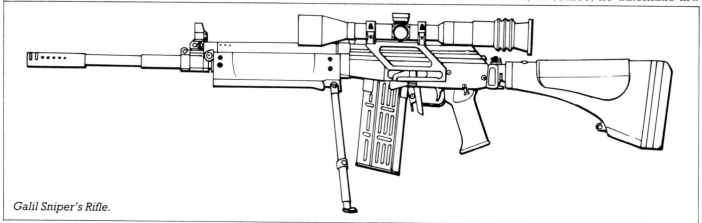

Galil Sniper's Rifle.

option; the trigger is a carefully assembled two-stage mechanism giving a graduated pull and crisp release. The butt folds for ease of carriage, and locks very rigidly when in the firing position. It carries a cheek-piece which is adjustable for height, and spacers can be placed beneath the rubber recoil pad to adjust for length.

There is a very rigid telescope mount assembled to the left side of the receiver by a quick-release system. The 6x40 telescope fits to this mount, and the telescope and mount can be quickly removed from the rifle and replaced without disturbing the zero point.

Each rifle is supplied in a specially-designed transit case which also carries the telescope and mount, optical filters for the telescope, firing and carrying slings, spare magazines and cleaning equipment. Using 7·62mm Match Grade ammunition, the Galil Sniper can easily place all its shots inside a 12cm circle at 300 metres range.

Specification:
Calibre: 7·62mm NATO
Operation: Gas, semi-automatic
Length: 1115mm (butt fixed);
840mm (butt folded)
Weight: 6·4kg

Barrel: 508mm without muzzle brake; 4 grooves, right-hand twist
Magazine: 20-round box
Muzzle velocity: 815 m/sec.

The Sniper is a selected Galil rifle in 7.62mm with special sights and other fittings.

123

Manufacturer: Pietro Beretta SpA, Gardone Val Trompia

In the early 1980s the Italian Army decided that it would replace the 7·62mm with 5·56mm weapons and issued a fairly broad specification, inviting manufacturers to submit designs. By this time Beretta had some field experience with their AR70/223 rifle and had found some minor deficiencies in the design, so they set about rectifying these to produce a suitable weapon for submission.

The receiver of the AR70/223 was a pressed steel box with the bolt guides pressed in, and in severe circumstances it had been found to distort sufficiently to jam the bolt. The receiver was therefore re-designed in a stronger form with welded-on bolt guide rails. The firing mechanism is designed to produce single shots, three-round bursts or automatic fire, and is so designed that it can be pre-set to give any two of these options. The weapon is gas operated, using a bolt carrier and rotating bolt driven by a gas piston. There is a carrying handle which can be easily removed to expose a telescope sight mount; the carrying handle mounting is pierced to give a through line of sight for the standard iron sights.

One of the most innovative things about this weapon is that the barrel is carefully manufactured with a collar which butts on to the receiver and so locates the chamber in the correct position in relation to the bolt, so that no adjustment for headspace is required when replacing a barrel. The barrel is retained in place by a threaded nut which clamps the collar tightly to the receiver face.

In addition to the standard rifle there is a carbine version, the **SC70/90**, which differs only in having a folding metal butt-stock. There is also a Special Service Carbine, **SCS70/90** which has the same folding butt-stock and also a shorter barrel. The rifle and carbine have their muzzle shaped for grenade launching and are capable of shutting off the gas regulator when firing

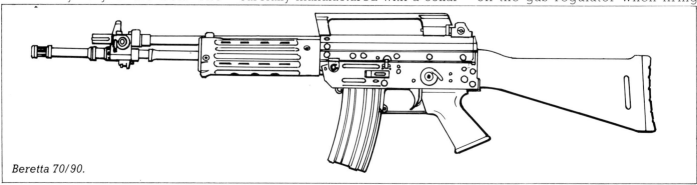

Beretta 70/90.

grenades. There is also a heavy-barrelled version of the rifle which is intended for use as the squad light automatic.

The rifle was submitted for trial in 1985, together with three other designs from different manufacturers. In June 1990 it was approved for adoption by the Italian armed forces.

Beretta incorporated lessons from earlier designs into the AR70/90. Top: the standard length rifle with fixed butt. Below: the carbine version with butt folded.

Specification (AR70/90):

Calibre: 5·56mm NATO
Operation: Gas, selective fire
Length: 998mm
Weight: 3·99kg
Barrel: 450mm, 6 grooves, right-hand twist
Magazine: 30-round box
Rate of fire: 600 rds/min. (estimated)
Muzzle velocity: 900 m/sec.

BERETTA AR70/·223   Italy

Manufacturer: Pietro Beretta SpA, Gardone Val Trompia

In the 1970s the 5·56mm cartridge began to assume an important place in the world's armouries, and the Pietro Beretta company considered it was time that they offered a rifle in this calibre; they were also alert to the fact that by that time the 7·62mm BM59 rifle was becoming obsolete and that there was a strong movement towards re-arming in 5·56mm calibre.

The **Beretta AR70/·223** rifle was a light, gas-operated weapon using a rotating bolt and capable of delivering either single shots or full-automatic fire. Lke most other 5·56mm rifles of the time it made extensive use of steel pressings and welding, and the butt, pistol grip and fore-end were of plastic material. The principal structure was welded, and component parts were attached by spring catches and removeable pins. The muzzle was formed into a combination of flash hider and grenade launcher, and a special folding front sight was fitted for aiming grenades. This sight was connected to the gas regulator; when lifted to take aim, the sight automatically cut off the supply of gas to the piston, so that the breech did not

open and all the gas generated by the special grenade-launching cartridge was delivered to the base of the grenade toobtain the maximum range.

The **AR70/·223** was the standard rifle with a 450mm barrel. A version for mechanised troops was the **SC70**, similar in general design but with a folding metal butt-stock. A third version, designed for use by airborne or commando troops requiring a more compact weapon, was the **SC70 Short**, which had a 320mm barrel with the same folding butt-stock.

Although tested by the Italian Army the AR70 family was not generally

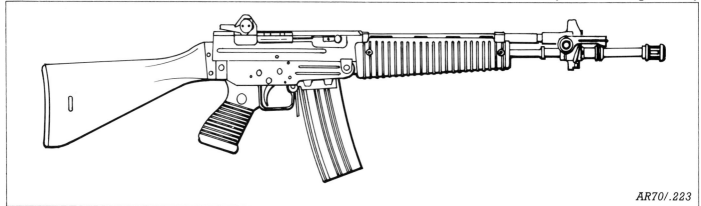

AR70/.223

adopted, though numbers were taken into use by Italian Special Forces units. It was then sold to Jordan and Malaysia and some other countries.

Top: The SC70/.223 with first-pattern butt.
Below: The AR70/.223 was Beretta's first venture into the 5.56mm assault rifle field, and though adopted in small numbers, it was too early for the Italian Army: but it gave Beretta the chance to learn useful lessons before they designed the 70/90 model.

Specification:
Calibre: 5·56mm M193
Operation: Gas, selective fire
Length: 955mm
Weight: 3·50kg
Barrel: 450mm, 4 grooves, right-hand twist
Magazine: 30-round box
Rate of fire: 650 rds/min.
Muzzle velocity: 950 m/sec.

BERETTA SNIPER

Italy

Manufacturer: Pietro Beretta SpA, Gardone Val Trompia

This is a conventional bolt-action magazine rifle, using a modified form of Mauser bolt with front locking lugs. The heavy barrel is free-floating in the stock and is fitted with a flash hider. A tube beneath the barrel, mostly concealed within the stock, is attached to the receiver and contains an harmonic balancer, a weight and springs which tend to remain in the same spatial position during recoil and thus damp out the vibrations of the barrel which produce inaccurate and

inconsistent shooting. The end of this tube is also used to mount the folding bipod, and it also carries a sliding hand-stop which can be used as a forward attachment point for a sling.

The high quality wooden stock has a thumb-hole, for a comfortable grip, and is fitted with a cheek-piece which can be adjusted for height so that the firer's face always takes up the same position relative to the sights. There is a rubber recoil pad on the end of the butt which is capable of being removed, and between it and the butt spacers can be inserted so as to fit the

length of the butt to the firer's reach.
The standard sights are of target-shooting quality; the front sight is a blade protected by a hood which also prevents reflections from the blade. The rear sight is a V-notch which is capable of adjustment for elevation and windage. As a sniping rifle, though, it is to be expected that a telescope sight will be used and the receiver has dovetail sight mounts in front of and behind the loading aperture. The manufacturers recommend, and fit as standard, the Zeiss Diavari-Z telescope, which has

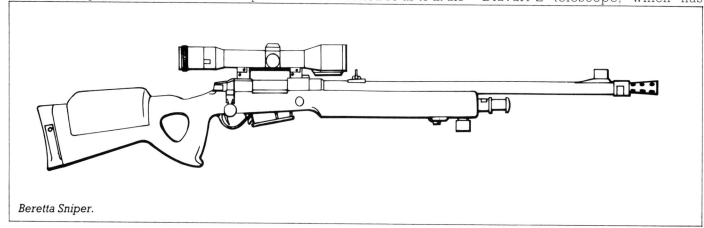

Beretta Sniper.

variable zoom magnification from 1·5x to 6x and can be provided with a variety of graticules matched to the ammunition. The sight mount is to the NATO STANAG 2324 and thus when the telescope is removed any NATO-standard night vision sight or other optical sight can be fitted in its place. The Beretta Sniper has been adopted by a number of European police forces and by armies in other parts of the world.

Specification:
Calibre: 7·62mm NATO
Operation: Manual, single-shot
Length: 1165mm
Weight: 5·55kg empty without sights or bipod
Barrel: 586mm, 4 grooves, right-hand twist
Magazine: 5-round box
Muzzle velocity: 845m/sec.

Like many other armies, the Italians prefer a bolt-action rifle for their sniping weapon, and the Beretta also uses a traditional wooden stock instead of the fashionable plastic.

NM149S SNIPER'S RIFLE Norway

Manufacturer: Våpensmia A/S, Dokka

The Norwegians, like the Swiss, have always had a high regard for individual marksmanship, and a good sniping rifle has always been an important part of the Norwegian Army's inventory. They retained the Krag-Jørgensen rifle as a sniper until after 1945, many years after every other user of the Krag had scrapped it, and after that they adopted Mausers. In 1988 they adopted the **NM149S**, manufactured by a small company specialising in target weapons and shooting equipment.

The **NM149S** uses a modified Mauser Model 1898 bolt action, generally conceded to be the most secure and precise bolt action ever made. This is allied to a cold-forged heavy barrel, and the entire unit is bedded into a stock fabricated from 28 layers of beech veneer which is chemically impregnated with resin to give strength and make the wood entirely proof against moisture and warping in service. There are two designs of stock; the military version is the more slender of the two, and the police version, in addition to being deeper, is provided with a cheek-piece which

can be adjusted for height. Both types of stock have a synthetic butt-plate, and the length of the butt can be adjusted by removing the butt-plate and adding one or two spacer blocks.

The trigger is of target match specification and is adjustable for pull. the magazine is a five-shot box which is removed from the bottom of the rifle for reloading, since the low-set sights prevent loading from the top of the action.

The rifle is fitted with two sets of sights. The primary sight is a telescope which mounts on to a steel bar running across the top of the receiver above the

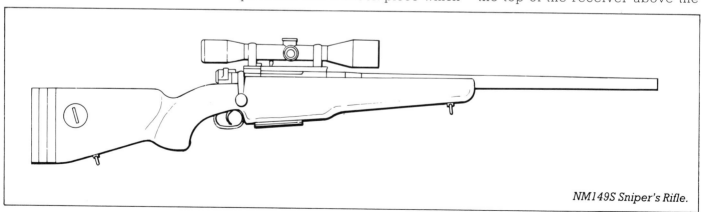

NM149S Sniper's Rifle.

130

boltway; in this position, although it prevents loading the magazine, it does not interfere with ejection of the fired case. The standard telescope is a Schmidt & Bender 6x42 which is adjustable for ranges from 100 to 800 metres. Alternatively, a 4x36 or a 6x42 zoom telescope can be supplied. The telescope fits on to the mount bar with a quick-release which allows instant removal and replacement without affecting zero. The secondary sight is an adjustable aperture rear sight attached to the sight mount bar, and a blade foresight, both of which can be adjusted for zero to any desired range.

Specification:
Calibre: 7·62mm NATO
Operation: Manual, single-shot
Length: 1120mm
Weight, empty: 5·6kg with telescope
Barrel: 600mm, 4 grooves, right-hand twist
Magazine: 5-shot detachable box
Muzzle velocity: 838 m/sec.

By using a very heavy and stiff barrel, allied to a thoroughly reliable bolt action, the NM149S produces exceptional accuracy out to long ranges and withstands climatic extremes.

SR88 ASSAULT RIFLE   # Singapore

Manufacturer: Chartered Firearms Industries Pte Ltd

The **SR88** is an improved version of the SAR80 in most respects. The lower receiver is an aluminium forging, reducing the weight without impairing the rigidity of the assembly, and the bolt carrier and bolt use a similar double-rod support system to that used on the earlier rifle. The gas cylinder is above the barrel, and it, the piston and the gas regulator are all chromium-plated to reduce wear and prevent the build-up of gas fouling during prolonged firing. The upper receiver is a steel pressing, and the barrel is cold-forged steel with a chromium-plated chamber. The barrel is fitted with a flash suppressor which vents sideways and upwards, and is internally threaded to accept a blank-firing attachment. The barrel is attached to the receiver by a key and locknut, a system which simplifies assembly and allows for rapid field replacement of a damaged barrel without the need for long adjustment of the cartridge headspace. The hand-guard has been designed so that the US M203 grenade launcher can easily be fitted to the rifle without modification.

The firing pin is provided with a spring which keeps the pin to the rear of the bolt except when struck by the firing hammer. This feature is a safety device which prevents the firing pin being flung forward and firing a sensitive cap if the rifle is accidentally dropped or struck. The firing mechanism provides for single shots and either automatic fire or three-round bursts, according to the purchaser's wishes. The cocking handle has an automatic lock to provide for positive and silent bolt closing.

The fixed butt is of glass-reinforced nylon. There is also a version in which the butt is formed of two lightweight tubes, hinged to the rear of the receiver so that it can fold sideways

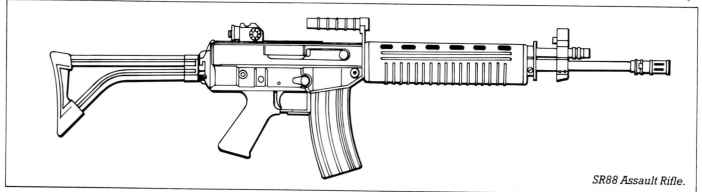

SR88 Assault Rifle.

and lie alongside the receiver. The length of either type of butt can be adjusted by removing the butt-plate and pad and inserting spacers.

A carbine version, with a shorter barrel, is also available in fixed or folding butt configuration. All versions are fitted with a fully adjustable rear sight, and both rear and front sights have luminous spots for aiming assistance in poor light. In addition, the upper receiver is formed into a dovetail for mounting any type of optical sight or night vision sight.

Singapore began rifle production by building the M16 under license; the SR88 adopted a similar bolt mechanism but the remainder is of their own design. Here are the standard and carbine versions, both with tubular folding butt.

Specification:
Calibre: 5·56mm NATO
Operation: Gas, selective fire
Length: 970mm
Weight: 3·66kg
Barrel: 459mm, 6 grooves, right-hand twist
Magazine: 20- or 30-round box
Rate of fire: 750 rds/min.
Muzzle velocity: 970 m/sec.

KALASHNIKOV AK & AKM

Soviet Union

**Manufacturer: State arsenals
(Variants: AK, AKS, AKM, AKMS, AKM-SU)**

The Kalashnikov has become one of the world's most popular weapons, serving regular forces with and without pro-Communist leanings and countless terrorist groups.

Production is said to have topped 70 million guns, and was undertaken in many former Soviet bloc countries – in particular, Bulgaria, East Germany, Hungary, Poland, Romania, Yugoslavia – and also in the People's Republic of China. Modified guns have even emanated from Finland, Israel and South Africa.

The Kalashnikov action taps propellant gas at the mid-point of the bore to strike a piston attached to the bolt carrier. This drives the piston/bolt carrier assembly backward and rotates the bolt out of engagement.

Most rifles have wood butts and fore-ends, with pistol grips that were originally laminated wood but later became coarsely chequered or ribbed plastic. The receiver was extended in the early 1950s to receive the tip of the butt, reducing the number of breakages, and shallow panels were milled in the sides of the receiver to save weight. Butt plates are steel, with a hinged

trap, and a cleaning rod is carried beneath the barrel.

The **AKS** variant, particularly popular with airborne forces and armoured-vehicle crewmen, has a pressed-steel butt that folds down and forward under the receiver.

The **AKM** is essentially a 'product improved' AK, introduced in 1959 once appropriate metalworking techniques had been mastered. The receiver is a sturdy U-shape pressing, much lighter than the machined forging of the AK. The bolt-lock recesses are riveted in place, and the receiver cover (also a pressing) is prominently ribbed.

The gas-piston tube has

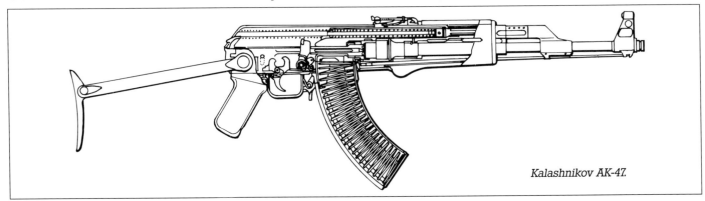

Kalashnikov AK-47.

semi-circular vents immediately behind the gas-port assembly instead of the circular holes on the AK, and the bolt carrier is phosphated. The charging handle and pistol grip are made of plastic, though the butt and fore-end are usually laminated wood.

The AKM introduced a 'rate-reducer' in the trigger system, which held the hammer back after the bolt-carrier had depressed the safety sear and thus reduced the rate of fire by about 15 per cent. A short oblique-cut compensator was added in the early 1960s to prevent the gun climbing to the right when firing automatically, and the fore-end was broadened to improve grip.

A bracket was eventually added on the left side of the receiver to accept infra-red or image-intensifier sights. Some rifles have single-shot grenade launchers under the fore-end, grenade-launching sights above the gas tube, and special butt pads to minimise the effects of recoil. A few guns have been adapted for the PBS-1 silencer, which relies on a rubber plug and a series of baffle plates to reduce noise. These AKM can be recognised by the back-sight leaf, which is adapted for special subsonic ammunition.

The AKMS replaced the AKS. It has a distinctive folding butt, with three rivets and a long flute on each side of the strut, which swings down and forward. Made only in 1975–79, the compact AKM-SU has a 35cm barrel and a simple rocking-L back sight combined with the receiver-cover pivot. A chequered plastic pistol grip accompanies a short wooden thumb-hole fore-end; a short finned muzzle chamber has a conical flash-hider; and the front sight block abuts the barrel guard.

AK magazines were originally plain-sided, but these proved to be too weak and ribs were soon added to increase body-strength; the earliest AKM magazines were ribbed sheet-metal, but these gave way to orange-red plastic patterns.

Widely criticised for its clumsiness, low muzzle velocity and an inefficient cartridge, the Kalashnikov is also simple, solid, reliable, and surprisingly effective when firing automatically. Details of the many copies of the AK series may be found in the Greenhill Military Manual, *Kalashnikov*.

Specification (AKM):
Calibre: 7.62mm Soviet M43
Operation: Gas operated, selective fire
Length: 878mm
Weight, without magazine: 3.85kg
Barrel: 415mm, 4 grooves, right-hand twist
Magazine: 30-round box
Rate of fire: 650 rds/min
Muzzle velocity: 710 m/sec

The standard AKM with fixed wooden butt.

KALASHNIKOV AK-74   Soviet Union/Russia

Manufacturer: State factories (Variants: AK-74, AK-74M, AK-74UB, AKS-74, AKS-74U, AKS-74Y, 'Hundred Series')

Experiments with 5.56mm M16 rifles captured in Vietnam convinced the Soviets that their 7.62mm cartridge was obsolescent. A 5.45mm derivative appeared in the early 1970s, with a two-piece bullet. A hollow tip within the bullet jacket was intended to improve lethality by deforming against a target.

The **AK-74** resembles the AKM, but (apart from the earliest examples) has synthetic furniture and an enlarged muzzle-brake/compensator with two angled ports to prevent the rifle climbing to the right during automatic fire. The sides of the butt are fluted to allow the calibre to be identified by touch, and lugs beneath the barrel accept an improved bayonet. The **AKS-74**, popular with parachutists and vehicle crews, has a triangular skeletal butt that folds back along the left side of the receiver.

The **AK-74M** was a 1980s universal-issue replacement for the AK-74 and the AKS-74. Its conventionally-shaped butt, locked in the extended position with a special cam-latch, swings forward along the left side of the receiver to reduce overall length. Furniture is plastic, and a rail on the left side of the receiver accepts optical, passive infra-red or intensifier sights. Guns are usually given an 'N' designation suffix (e.g., AK-74N, AKS-74UN).

The short-barrelled **AKS-74U**, which superseded the AKMS-U in 1979, measures 675mm overall (butt extended) and weighs only about 2.7kg. The rocking-L back sight is retained, but pressing a catch on the left side of the receiver behind the pistol grip allows an AKS-74-type skeletal butt to fold back along the

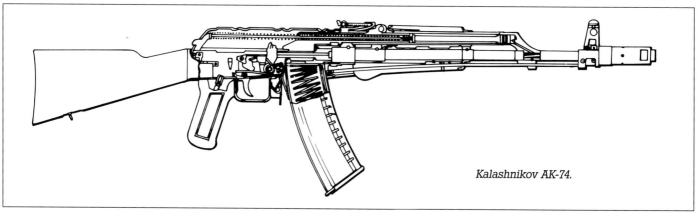

Kalashnikov AK-74.

receiver. The AKS-74U also has a short cylindrical barrel extension.

The **AK-74UB** was derived from the AK-74 in the late 1970s to fire a noiseless SP-3 'piston seal' cartridge, and the **AKS-74Y** has a semi-integral silencer attached to its shortened barrel, the fore-end and barrel casing being cut-back accordingly.

A modified AK-74M entered in the Russian Army trials of the early 1990s provided the basis for the 'Hundred Series' Kalashnikovs announced in 1995. These include the **AK101**, chambered for the 5.56x45mm round, which has a burst-firing capability, a refined muzzle-brake/compensator unit, and minor improvements to the plastic furniture.

The **AK103** is identical except for its chambering (7.62x39mm) and curved magazine, whereas the **AK105** accepts the 5.45x39mm pattern.

The **AK102** and **AK104** are short-barrelled derivatives of the AK101 and AK103 respectively, comparable with the AKM-SU, with a short flash-hider and a simplified 300m (330yd) sight carried on an extension of the back-sight block..

It has been stated that the AN-94 (Nikonov) assault rifle will replace the Kalashnikov in Russian service as and when funds permit, but the Izhevsk factory clearly believes that the Kalashnikov has a future.

Specification (AK-74):

Calibre: 5.45mm Soviet M74
Operation: Gas, selective fire
Length: 956mm
Weight: 4.85kg with loaded magazine
Barrel: 415mm, 4 grooves, right-hand twist
Magazine: 30- or 40-round box
Rate of fire: 650 rds/min
Muzzle velocity: 900 m/sec

The AK-74 is simply the basic AK-47 re-designed so as to fire a reduced calibre 5.45mm cartridge, a move which followed the US adoption of the 5.56mm cartridge. Note the adoption of a muzzle brake to improve accuracy in automatic fire.

SIMONOV CARBINE (SKS)   # Soviet Union

Manufacturer: State Arsenals

Sergei Simonov was a skilled Soviet weapon designer who, as early as 1936, had provided the Red Army with an automatic rifle and followed it with an anti-tank rifle in 1941. By this time the Soviets were experimenting with short cartridges, though they dropped the idea for some time after the German invasion. Then, in 1943, the German 7·92mm Short cartridge was deployed against them and they went back to their project and developed the 7·62x39mm M1943 cartridge. Simonov was given the task of providing a suitable automatic rifle to fire it.

The **Simonov SKS** rifle did not appear until after the war, and within ten years was superseded by the Kalashnikov weapons, but it was retained as a ceremonial rifle, in reserve, and was manufactured by several Communist countries including East Germany, China, North Korea and Yugoslavia for many years. It is a simple and robust weapon, easy to operate and maintain, which is probably the reason for its long life.

The breech closure system was adapted by Simonov from his wartime anti-tank rifle design. The bolt is rectangular in section and is held inside a bolt carrier; the carrier has shaped ramps which control the movement of the bolt. Above the barrel is a gas cylinder containing a piston and rod; on firing, gas is vented into the cylinder to drive the piston rod back. It strikes the front of the bolt carrier and starts it moving backwards. The ramps in the carrier lift the rear end of the bolt clear from a recess in the floor of the receiver, and then the bolt is carried back against the pressure of a spring, extracting the fired case. The return spring then drives the carrier back, the bolt strips a round from the magazine and pushes

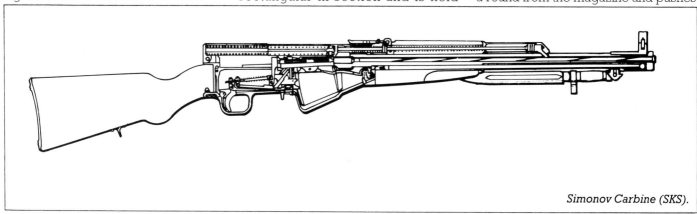

Simonov Carbine (SKS).

it into the chamber. As the bolt stops, tight against the cartridge, the carrier continues to move forward for a short distance and the ramps now force the rear end back down into the locking recess. A hammer fires the cartridge by means of a firing pin in the bolt.

The magazine is inside the stock and is loaded by a charger through the open action; it can be hinged open from below to unload without having to cycle the bolt mechanism. As with most Soviet weapons of the time, the Simonov was given a permanently-attached bayonet which hinges back and lies in a slot in the fore-end.

Specification:
Calibre: 7·62mm M43
Operation: Gas, semi-automatic
Length: 1022mm
Weight: 3·86kg
Barrel: 520mm, 4 grooves, right-hand twist
Magazine: 10-round integral box
Muzzle velocity: 735 m/sec.

The Simonov was the first Soviet rifle to use the M1943 short 7.62mm cartridge, but it was soon superseded by the AK47. Nevertheless, it was widely exported and copied in several Communist countries.

CETME MODELS L and LC   # Spain

**Manufacturer: Empresa Nacional
'Santa Barbara', Madrid**

In the aftermath of World War II
several German weapon designers
and technicians made their way to
Spain, taking with them their
knowledge of many wartime German
development programmes. Some
went to work for a Spanish government
arms development 'think-tank' called
CETME (Company for Technical
Studies of Special Materials), and when
CETME were called upon to develop a
modern rifle for the Spanish Army,

they resurrected a Mauser design for
an assault rifle known as the
Sturmgewehr 45 which had been
brought to a halt by the end of the war.
The important feature of this rifle was
its bolt design. The rifle was a delayed
blowback weapon, intended for the
short 7·92mm cartridge, and adopted a
two-piece bolt separated by two
rollers. As the bolt closed, the heavy
rear section forced the rollers
outwards into recesses in the receiver.
When the rifle was fired, the pressure
forced the cartridge back and pushed

the light bolt head against the rollers,
trying to force them out of the
recesses. To move, the rollers had, in
turn, to push back the bolt body at a
considerable mechanical disadvan-
tage. They eventually perfected this
design, which was later adopted by
Heckler & Koch for their series of rifles.
The CETME Model A was the first rifle
to appear, but this had technical
drawbacks and was succeeded by the
Models B and C, the latter being
adopted in 7·62mm calibre as the
Spanish Army rifle. When, in the late

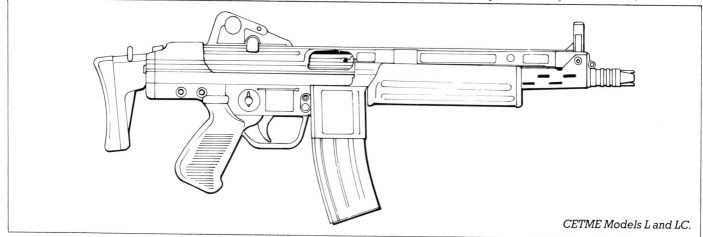

CETME Models L and LC.

1970s, the Spanish Army decided to go to 5·56mm, the design was overhauled and the result was the **CETME Model L**.

The **Model L** is a modern assault rifle, with a pressed-steel receiver and plastic furniture. The bolt mechanism is the same roller-locked delayed blow-back pioneered in the Model A, though slightly improved in minor details over the years. First models had a three-round burst facility and used a 20-round magazine, but these weapons were soon dropped and the service version has the option of single shots or automatic fire and uses the M16 type of magazine interface. The **Model L** is a fixed-butt weapon, standard for most of the Army. The **Model LC** is a short-barrelled (320mm) version with a butt formed from two metal arms which telescope in alongside the receiver for compactness, and is used by airborne and some mechanised troops. Both models began entering Spanish Army service in 1988.

Specification (Model L):

Calibre: 5·56mm NATO
Operation: Delayed blowback, selective fire
Length: 925mm
Weight: 3·40kg
Barrel: 400mm, 6 grooves, right-hand twist
Magazine: 30-round box
Rate of fire: 700 rds/min.
Muzzle velocity: 875 m/sec.

A member of the Spanish Special Forces using a CETME Model L rifle fitted with telescope sight. The drawing (left) shows the Model LC carbine with collapsible butt.

STURMGEWEHR 57 (StGw.57) **Switzerland**

Manufacturer: Schweizerische Industrie Gesellschaft, Neuhausen-Rheinfalls

The Schweizerische Industrie Gesellschaft (SIG) have been manufacturing rifles for the Swiss Army since 1869, and in the intervening years they have also developed submachine guns and machine guns, as well as a highly respected line of pistols. They have always had a finger on the pulse of current arms development, and after 1945 they looked closely at many designs which the war had thrown up, among them the Mauser Sturmgewehr 45, a design which was never completed before the war ended. This used an unusual roller locked breech mechanism, and SIG took this idea and developed it into a practical mechanism, applying it to a rifle which they then offered to the Swiss Army. After trial it was adopted as the **Sturmgewehr 57**, and has remained in use ever since; most first-line Swiss units have now re-equipped with the 5.56mm StG.90, but reservists and second-line formations still use the StGw.57.

The most immediately obvious feature of the StGw.57 is the 'straight line' layout, the axis of the barrel and the top of the butt lying in a perfectly straight line. This means that the recoil force passes straight down the weapon and into the shoulder; weapons with conventionally sloped butts drive the recoil force back some inches above the point of contact with the shoulder and thus the rifle tends to lift the muzzle at each shot. The StGw.57 is remarkably steady and very accurate.

The bolt mechanism is in two parts, a light head and a heavy body, with two rollers separating the units. As the bolt closes, the nose of the body forces the rollers out and locks them into recesses in the receiver. On firing, the bolt head tends to set back, but it cannot open due to the rollers; pressure on the rollers is

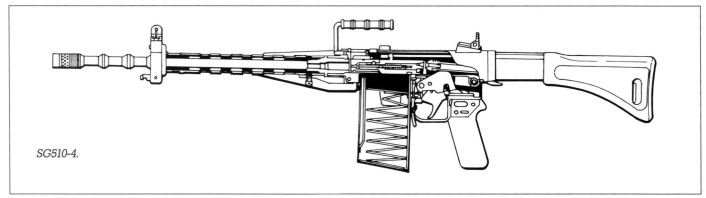

SG510-4.

transmitted to the bolt body, and is assisted by a controlled leak of gas around the cartridge and through holes in the bolt head, which impinges on the bolt body. These two forces combine to move the bolt body back, so leaving room for the rollers to be forced inwards by the bolt head, and eventually the rollers come free from the recesses and the bolt opens.

The **StGw.57** is provided with a folding bipod, and it is also possible to launch grenades from the muzzle. However, though the Swiss Army was satisfied with the design, SIG elected to make changes. The resulting **SG510** series comprised the **SG510-1**, a 7.62mm NATO version of the 7.5mm StGw.57; the lightweight 7.62mm **SG510-2**; the **SG510-3**, made in small numbers for the Soviet 7.62mm M43 cartridge; and the 7.62mm NATO **SG510-4**, introduced in 1963, which was bought in quantity by Chile. However, the conflict between firearms manufacture and stringent Swiss arms-exporting laws prevented large-scale success, and the rise of the 5.56mm cartridge led instead to the small-calibre **SG530** and then to the **SG540** series (5.56mm and 7.62mm).

Specification (StGw.57):
Calibre: 7.5mm Swiss
Operation: Delayed blowback, selective fire
Length: 1105mm
Weight: 5.55kg
Barrel: 583mm, 4 grooves, right-hand twist
Magazine: 24-round box
Rate of fire: 450–500 rds/min
Muzzle velocity: 760 m/sec

Although somewhat heavy by today's standards, the StGw.57 is accurate and reliable, and will remain in reserve in Switzerland for many years to come. These photographs show the commercial 7.62mm derivatives, the standard SIG SG510-1 (above) and lightweight SG510-2 (top).

143

ASSAULT RIFLE SG550 — Switzerland

Manufacturer: Schweizerische Industrie Gesellschaft, Neuhausen-Rheinfalls
(Variant Model: SGS51)

SIG continued development of rifles after the SG510 series, following it with the SG540 which was made under licence in France and sold widely throughout the world. Then, in the late 1970s, the Swiss Army asked for a design to fire the 5.56mm cartridge, and SIG produced the **SG550**. A competitive trial was held, the other entrant being a design from the Swiss Federal Arms Factory, and in 1983 the SG550 was selected for adoption. Unfortunately, due to financial problems and the priority to provide some new tanks, the

introduction of the new rifle was delayed until 1986 when it went into service as the **StG.90**.

The SG550 uses a conventional gas cylinder and piston driving a bolt carrier containing a rotating bolt. The hammer firing mechanism is capable of providing single shots, three-round bursts or automatic fire. The magazine is translucent so that the contents can be checked, and has studs on one side and sockets on the other so that two or three magazines can be clipped together. This allows any one magazine to be used, and when this is empty it is simply a matter of pulling the empty magazine free, shifting the set sideways and pushing the next magazine into place.

Plastics are used for the butt and fore end, and the butt can be folded sideways to lie alongside the receiver. There is a light metal bipod which folds up beneath the fore-end when not required.

The standard sights are an aperture rear sight, fully adjustable for windage and elevation, and a hooded blade foresight which can be height-adjusted for zeroing. The sights have luminous spots for aiming in poor light and these are part of the movable portion of the sight, so that adjustment of the day sight also adjusts the night sights. In addition, the top of the receiver is formed into a telescope mount to fit the standard Swiss Army optical and night vision sights; for export

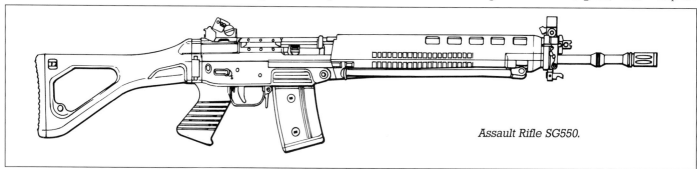

Assault Rifle SG550.

purposes, the NATO standard sight base can be fitted if required.

The **SG551** is similar to the SG550 but is a shorter carbine model with a 372mm barrel. The **SG550P** and **SG551SP** are commercial versions of the SG550 and SG551 respectively. They are capable only of semi-automatic fire, and are made so that they cannot be illegally converted back to fully automatic operation.

An ultra-compact **SG551LB** 'sub-carbine' and a **SSG550** sniper-rifle derivative have also been offered. The rifle has a heavy barrel, a bipod, and an anatomical pistol grip with an adjustable palm-rest. Optical sights are standard, and non-reflective 'mirage bands' are usually fitted.

Specification (SG550):
Calibre: 5.56mm
Operation: Gas, selective fire
Length: 998mm butt extended; 772mm butt folded
Weight: 4.1kg with magazine & bipod
Barrel: 528mm, 6 grooves, right-hand twist
Magazine: 20- or 30-round box
Rate of fire: 700 rds/min
Muzzle velocity: 995 m/sec

Top right: SG550 standard rifle fitted with an experimental red dot sight.

Above right: The standard-issue StG90 complete with accessories.

145

ENFIELD SA80 (L85A1)

Manufacturer: Royal Small Arms Factory, Nottingham

Development of this rifle began in 1972 and it was first shown publicly in 1976. At that time it was built in 4.85mm calibre to suit a new cartridge developed specifically for this weapon. In 1977–80 the rifle and cartridge went through extensive NATO trials to determine the future NATO cartridge; the result was the adoption of the 5.56mm cartridge as standard, and the Enfield rifle therefore had to be redesigned in this calibre. This was not so hard as

might be imagined, since the designers were alert to the possibility and had taken this into account in the initial design. A number of other modifications, resulting from experience gained in the trial, were incorporated into the design and it was finally introduced into British Army service in 1985.

The **L85A1** is a bullpup rifle, the action being set well back in the stock so as to give a compact overall length and yet have the maximum barrel length. The mechanism is a straightforward gas-piston-operated rotating bolt in a bolt carrier, the

carrier riding on rods inside the receiver. The standard infantry rifle is provided with the 'SUSAT' optical sight giving 4x magnification, with a small emergency open sight forming part of the optical sight casing. Non-infantry units are issued with a rifle having a carrying handle in place of the optical sight and with conventional iron sights.

Variant models include a **Cadet** rifle which fires only single shots and which can be converted to .22 rimfire calibre; and a carbine version with short barrel. The L85A1 rifle is partnered by the **L86A1 Light**

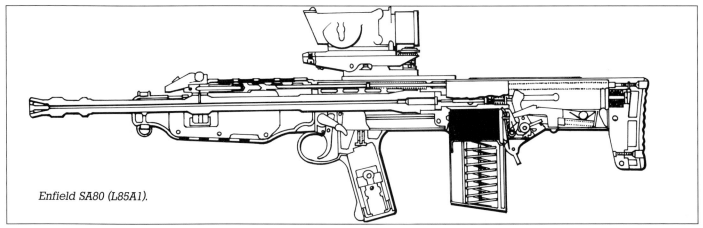

Enfield SA80 (L85A1).

Support Weapon, a heavy-barrelled version of the rifle for use as the squad light machine gun.

Unfortunately the introduction of the Enfield system was followed by complaints from troops of defective weapons, magazines falling out, handguards falling off and sights which failed to keep their alignment. Much of this was exaggerated, and such teething troubles occur in all new weapons, but there can be no doubt that far too many bad rifles reached the troops.

In the course of closing down the Royal Small Arms Factory at Enfield and moving the rifle-making facility to the Royal Ordnance Factory, Nottingham, the opportunity was taken to re-equip with entirely new machine tools, and the quality of rifles produced since late 1988 is better. However, complaints were raised again during the Gulf War of 1991 and British participation in peace-keeping missions in the Balkans.

An improved **L85A2** was accepted in 2002, but suspicion lingers; the Army is clearly unwilling to accept that the entire project has been a disaster. Whether the 'A2' performs any better than its predecessor remains to be seen.

Specification (L85A1):
Calibre: 5.56mm NATO
Operation: Gas, selective fire
Length: 785mm
Weight: 4.98kg with loaded magazine and sight
Barrel: 518mm, 6 grooves, right-hand twist
Magazine: 30-round box
Rate of fire: 940 rds/min
Muzzle velocity: 845 m/sec

The British Army first essayed a bullpup rifle in the EM1 and EM2 of the late 1940s but was politically defeated by NATO. The L85 adopted the same principle but used a simpler mechanism. The infantry rifle is fitted with the SUSAT optical sight, while the remainder of the army uses iron-sighted weapons.

RIFLE L96A1

Manufacturer: Accuracy International Ltd, Portsmouth

In the early 1980s the British Army began seeking a new sniping rifle; since the adoption of the FN-FAL as the service rifle, it had retained Lee-Enfield bolt-action rifles for sniping, but it was now time for a new weapon. Several models were extensively tested and the final selection was the **'Model PM Sniper'** made by Accuracy International, which was taken into service in 1986 as the **L96A1**.

The design is quite innovative; instead of the traditional wooden stock, the rifle is assembled to an aluminium frame which is then surrounded by a stock made of high-impact plastic material. This form of construction ensures that the rifle remains rigid even if the stock is struck or damaged, and so long as the frame is intact the rifle can still be used efficiently. Furthermore this form of construction does away with traditional methods of fixing and bedding barrels and actions into conventional

stocks, making repair and maintenance much easier.

The stainless steel barrel is screwed into an extended receiver, which gives added support, and a locking ring, formed with lugs, is screwed tightly against the barrel. The three bolt lugs pass through this ring and, when the bolt is turned, lock behind the lugs; the bolt handle provides a fourth lug as it locks into the receiver. This locking ring simplifies manufacture and, when wear takes place and the cartridge

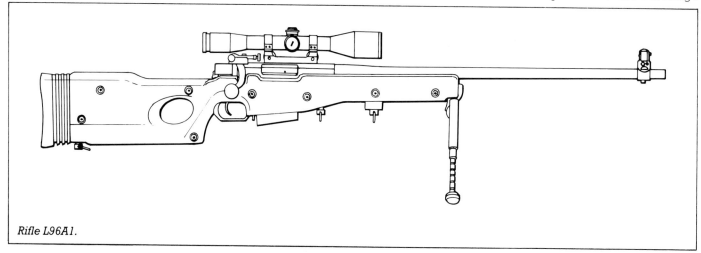

Rifle L96A1.

head clearance becomes excessive, a new ring can be fitted in a few minutes. Normal accuracy life of the barrel is well in excess of 5000 rounds.

The bolt operates in a 60° arc, two-thirds of the cocking action being performed during the opening stroke and the other third during the closing stroke, so evening out the bolt effort required. The firing pin travels only 6mm, ensuring a fast lock time.

The safety catch blocks the trigger, locks the bolt handle, and blocks the firing pin, totally preventing any accidental discharge even after violent blows.

There is a simple and robust telescope mount which allows the sight to be removed and replaced quickly without loss of zero. The standard telescope is either a Schmidt & Bender 10x42 or 2·5-10x56 zoom. Both are matched to a heavy match-grade bullet, and it is noticeable that the zoom telescope does not alter the point of impact as the zoom facility is used. Iron sights, capable of use to 700 metres range, are also fitted.

Specification:
Calibre: 7·62mm NATO
Operation: Manual, single-shot
Length: 1124-1194mm
Weight, empty: 6·50kg
Barrel: 655mm, 4 grooves, right-hand twist
Magazine: 10-round box
Muzzle velocity: 840 m/sec.

The L96A1 uses an aluminium 'chassis' to support the working parts, but clothes them in a plastic stock. The infantry version (left) has iron sights as standard; the special version below has no iron sights and a specially-designed flash hider.

BARRETT LIGHT FIFTY M82A1 USA

Manufacturer: Barrett Firearms Mfg. Co., Murfreesboro, Tenn.

In the early 1980s the idea arose of using heavy precision rifles in order to snipe against material targets at long range; the scenario on view was that of a deep-intrusion raiding party setting up in cover some 1500 metres away from a forward airfield and then, with a quick series of well-aimed shots, putting all the aircraft out of action. After which they would simply abandon the weapon and make their escape. Many similar scenarios can be envisaged.

The **Barrett Light Fifty** is one of these rifles, and is a semi-automatic weapon firing the standard ·50 Browning heavy machine gun cartridge. The barrel and bolt carrier recoil after firing for about 25mm, after which the bolt is unlocked. The barrel stops moving and the bolt carrier and bolt are allowed to continue back, opening the bolt and extracting the spent case. A return spring is compressed during this movement, and the spring then drives the bolt forward to chamber a fresh round. The bolt locks and then the barrel and bolt assembly run forward

to the firing position.

The heavy barrel is fitted with a muzzle brake which, together with the recoil movement allowed to the barrel, absorbs a good deal of the recoil force and enables the gun to be fired from the shoulder in moderate comfort. The accuracy of the standard machine gun cartridge is marginal in this role, but the gradual acceptance of this type of rifle has seen the development of precision ammunition which gives good accuracy. In addition, there are a number of cartridges which have been developed for the Browning with

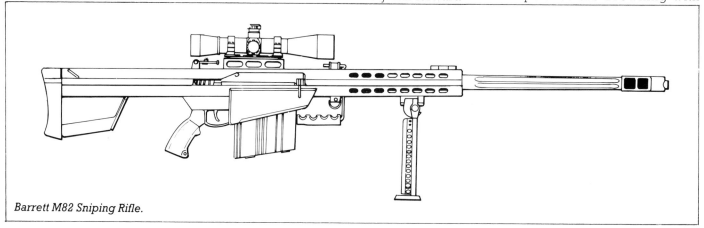

Barrett M82 Sniping Rifle.

considerable explosive and incendiary power, and using these will produce satisfactory results against the type of targets envisaged.

The **Light Fifty** is provided with an adjustable bipod, and it can also be fitted to most standard machine gun tripods. It is normally provided with a powerful telescope sight in order to allow use out to the maximum range of the ammunition, which can be up to 2000 metres, depending upon the type of target.

Specification:
Calibre: ·50 Browning
Operation: Short recoil, semi-automatic
Length: 1549mm
Weight: 14·7kg
Barrel: 838mm, 8 grooves, right-hand twist
Magazine: 11-round box
Muzzle velocity: 843 m/sec.

The Light Fifty uses the Browning .50 machine gun cartridge for long-range anti-materiel sniping. It is in use by US SEALs and by the British SAS.

US RIFLE M14

Manufacturers: Springfield Armory, Harrington & Richardson, Inc., the Winchester-Western Division of Olin Industries, and Thompson-Ramo-Woolridge, Inc. (Variants: M14, M15, M21)

The M1 Garand rifle, made in huge quantities, served the US Army extremely well during the Second World War. However, experience of perfected German and Soviet semi-automatic rifles, such as the Walther G. 43 and the Tokarev, showed that the quirky clip-loaded magazine (which prevented the addition of single cartridges) was a definite weakness.

The answer was found by refining the action of the experimental T44 rifle, created by combining the best features of the T20E2, T25 and T31. The new gun was tested successfully against the FN FAL (T48 to the US Army), and the **T44E4** was adopted as the 7.62mm **Rifle M14** in May 1957. The heavy-barrelled **T44E5** was also accepted as the **M15**.

The **M14** is essentially similar to the Garand rifle internally, though the detachable box magazine, shortened gas tube, and pistol-grip half-stock are most distinctive. The selector on many guns (unofficially known as 'M14M') will have been plugged to restrict them to semi-automatic fire, though a standard selector may be substituted if required.

The first production guns had wooden hand guards, but ventilated fibreglass-reinforced plastic soon became standard and lasted until the combination of a durable synthetic stock and a ribbed non-ventilated hand guard was approved.

Similar internally to the M14, the **M15** had a heavy barrel, a fixed-leg bipod attached to the gas cylinder, a strengthened stock, and a folding shoulder strap on the butt plate. Unfortunately, experience soon showed that the rifle was unsuited to the light support role, and it was declared obsolete in December 1959.

Work on the M14 ceased in 1963, and the production machinery was sold to the government of Taiwan in 1967. However, parts continued to be available. The M14 then proved itself in various practical-rifle shooting

Below: A commercial-type M14 rifle altered to approximate to M21 standards.

competitions and the renaissance of the design persuaded the US Army to investigate the M14 as a sniper-rifle. An XM21 derivative was successfully tested against the US Marine Corps' Remington 700 and guns imported from Europe, and conversion of National Match ('NM') pattern M14 rifles to XM21 standards began in Rock Island Arsenal in 1970. The XM21 was formally standardised in December 1975 as the **M21**, remaining so until the bolt-action 7.62mm Remington Model 24 was approved in 1987.

Though the 7.62mm M14 satisfied many US servicemen, there were many who believed (the magazine excepted) that it was inferior in quality and performance to the .30-06 Garand. Ironically, in 1957,

production of the M1 had begun in Italy, in a purpose-built Beretta factory in Rome.

The Italian Garands gave way to the 7.62mm **BM-59**, in much the same way that the M14 had replaced the M1 in US service. Many guns of this type were supplied to Indonesia and Nigeria, and smaller quantities have been distributed throughout the world.

Above: The Beretta BM-59 Mark IV.

Specification (M14):
Calibre: 7.62mm NATO
Operation: Gas, semi-automatic only
Length: 1125mm
Weight: 4.13kg with equipment and empty magazine
Barrel: 559mm, 4 grooves, right-hand twist
Magazine: 20-round box
Muzzle velocity: 853 m/sec

US RIFLE M16 USA

***Manufacturer: Colt's Patent
Firearms Mfg Co., Hartford, Conn.
(Variant Model: M16A1)***

During and after the Korean War the
US Operational Research Office
undertook long studies of the effective-
ness of rifle fire in combat; these led to
Project Salvo, in which various ways of
firing groups of small-calibre projec-
tiles were explored. Out of Project
Salvo came an Army request to the
ArmaLite Division of the Fairchild
Airplane and Engine Company to
develop a ·22 calibre military rifle,
since the Salvo trials and ORO studies

suggested that a small calibre would
produce casualties as well as a larger
calibre, and the small calibre meant
less recoil and less weight for the
soldier.

The result was the **ArmaLite AR-15**
rifle, developed by Eugene Stoner; it
ran into considerable opposition from
the US Army, but eventually some 8500
were purchased by the US Air Force,
and then, in 1963, it was adopted by
the army as the **M16**. After experience
in Vietnam the **M16A1** appeared in
1966; this adopted a positive bolt-
closing device to force cartridges into

a fouled chamber.

The **M16** uses an unusual gas system
of operation. Instead of the conventional gas piston, gas is tapped from
the barrel and led back into the
receiver by a tube which delivers the
gas blast directly to the bolt carrier and
thus blows it backwards. The bolt
carrier has a cam track engaging a lug
on the bolt, and as it moved, so it
rotates and unlocks the bolt, then
carries it back against the pressure of a
return spring. At the same time a
hammer mechanism is cocked. On the
return stroke of the bolt a round is

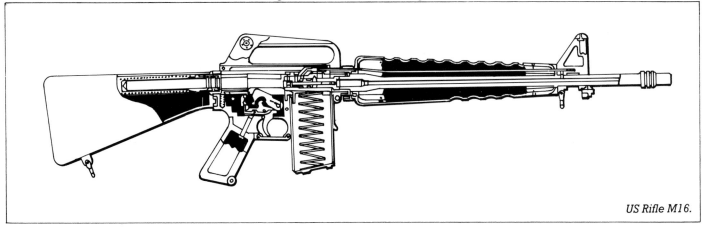

US Rifle M16.

driven from the magazine into the chamber, the bolt closes, and the remaining forward movement of the carrier rotates it to lock.

The system was designed around a particular type of propellant then in use by the US Army, but during the Vietnam war the specification for the propellant changed and this led to problems with the rifle. The bore and chamber were chromed, the bolt buffer changed to slow down the rate of automatic fire, and stricter instructions about cleaning were issued, which overcame the problem.

The **M16** (and **M16A1**) has been adopted by many other countries and has been manufactured under licence in Singapore, South Korea and the Philippine Republic. It is now being replaced in US service by the M16A2.

Specification:

Calibre: 5·56mm
Operation: Gas, selective fire
Length: 990mm
Weight: 2·86kg
Barrel: 508mm, 6 grooves, right-hand twist
Magazine: 30-round box
Rate of fire: 800 rds/min.
Muzzle velocity: 1000 m/sec.

The Colt/ArmaLite M16 is virtually the standard by which other assault rifles are compared. Capable of single shots or automatic fire it introduced the 5.56mm cartridge into military service.

**Manufacturer: Colt's
Manufacturing Co. Inc., Hartford,
Conn.**

In 1977-80 the NATO countries carried
out a long series of tests to settle on the
cartridge which would replace the
7·62mm as the future NATO standard.
The American 5·56mm, as used in the
M16A1, was a hot favourite and
eventually the 5·56mm cartridge was
selected, but with a new bullet
developed in Belgium known as the
SS109. This was longer and heavier
than the American M193 bullet and
therefore it required a different twist of
rifling in the barrel in order to perform
properly. It followed that the US Army
had either to re-barrel all its M16A1

rifles or find a new rifle suited to the
new cartridge. Colt were approached
with the problem, and they responded
by producing an improved M16 with a
heavier barrel. After some modification demanded by the Army, this was
adopted in 1983 as the **M16A2** and
has, by now, almost replaced the
M16A1 in US service.

The **M16A2** differs from its predecessor in several respects. The barrel is
heavier; but not entirely, since that part
beneath the fore-end had to remain the
same diameter as the M16A1 in order
to fit the attachment of the M203
grenade launcher, but heavy enough
to be stiffer and therefore more
accurate than that of the M16A1.

Instead of the full-automatic option of
the M16A1, the new rifle has a three-
round burst mechanism, a device
permitting three shots to be fired for
one trigger pressure. Since most
experienced troops fire short bursts in
automatic fire, this merely mechanises
the task and also prevents the rifle
climbing out of control in an over-long
burst. The barrel is, of course, rifled at
one turn in 7 inches so as to suit the
new standard bullet, and the rear sight
has been improved. A new flash
suppressor on the muzzle omits the
bottom slot of the earlier rifle, so
preventing dust being blown into the
air in prone firing and also eliminating
a rush of gas downwards which tended

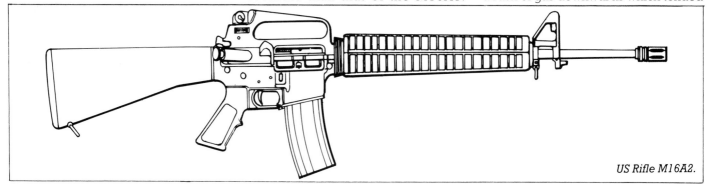

US Rifle M16A2.

to thrust the muzzle up. There is also a cartridge case deflector on the side of the receiver which directs the ejected case away from the face of a left-handed firer.

The **M16A2** has also been adopted by the Canadian Army as the **C7** rifle; in their case, the full-automatic option has been chosen instead of the three-round burst. There is also an **M16A2 Carbine**, with a shorter barrel and a collapsible butt; this is used by the Canadian Army as their **C8 Carbine**.

Specification:
Calibre: 5·56mm NATO
Operation: Gas, selective fire
Length: 1006mm
Weight: 3·58kg
Barrel: 508mm, 6 grooves, right-hand twist
Magazine: 30-round box
Rate of fire: 600-940 rds/min.
Muzzle velocity: 991 m/sec.

The M16A2 (top) has a heavier barrel, better sights, a cooler handguard, and a three-round burst-firing feature. It is regularly seen with sophisticated sights, such as the Magnavox infra-red sight, seen (above) on a standard M16A1.

US CARBINE M1

USA

Manufacturer: Winchester Repeating Arms Co; and others (Variant Models: M1A1, M2, M3)

In 1938 the US Army requested a light rifle for arming second-line troops and weapon crews who did not require a full-power rifle. The request was turned down, but was resubmitted in 1940 when several manufacturers were approached. A suitable cartridge was developed, and 11 competing designs were tested in May 1941. As it happened, the Winchester company had a light rifle in the course of development as a private venture and this, modified to meet the military specification, was accepted as the **Carbine M1** in September 1941.

The carbine uses a very similar bolt action to the Garand rifle, but the gas action is very different and was the first military application of what is now called a 'tappet' or 'short-stroke piston'. There is a short gas cylinder beneath the barrel which contains a captive piston. An operating rod, connected to the bolt by the same sort of curved plate and cam track as the Garand's, lies in contact with the piston. On firing, gas is vented into the cylinder and drives the light piston back very sharply, giving the operating rod an impulsive blow which is sufficient to drive it back and open the bolt. A return spring around the rod then pulls the bolt back to load the next round from a conventional box magazine. There is a hammer mechanism similar to that of the Garand to fire the cartridge.

As a short-range self-defence weapon the carbine was satisfactory, but the bullet is no more than a pistol bullet and at ranges over about 150 yards it is neither accurate nor very effective. Nevertheless, it was light and handy and became a popular weapon, several million being made by numerous contractors.

Soon after its introduction the **M1A1** appeared; this had a folding

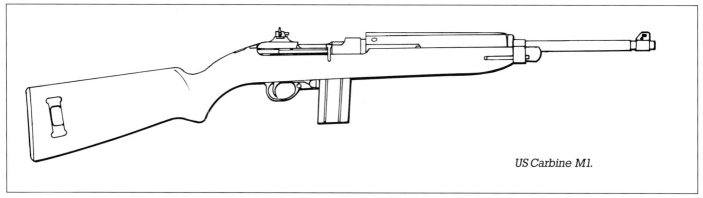

US Carbine M1.

metal butt and the weapon was intended for airborne and other troops who required a more compact weapon. Then came a demand for automatic fire, and the **M2** was introduced; this was precisely the same as the M1, but with the addition of a switch on the firing mechanism that allowed automatic fire. With this came a curved 30-round magazine to supplement the original 15-round magazine Finally, the **M3** was a special version of the M2 with fittings to take an infra-red night sight developed in 1944.

The manufacture of more than six million M1 Carbines during the Second World War allowed the US government to distribute hundreds of thousands of them to 'friendly' nations under the Offshore Programs of the 1950s and 1960s. Among the major beneficiaries were South Korea and Vietnam, recipients of nearly two million guns in 1950–75; 179,000 went to Taiwan, and 170,000 to the Netherlands, 159,000 to Italy, 155,000 to France and 98,000 to Norway.

Specification (M1):
Calibre: .30 Carbine M1
Operation: Gas, semi-automatic
Length: 905mm
Weight: 2.48kg
Barrel: 457mm, 4 grooves, right-hand twist
Magazine: 15- or 30-round box
Rate of fire: 750 rds/min (M2 and M3 only)
Muzzle velocity: 593 m/sec

The M1 Carbine was everybody's light and handy favourite weapon, and over six million were made between 1941 and 1945. Since then several commercial companies have made thousands of copies.

Glossary

Blowback

A type of automatic pistol in which the breech block or bolt is not positively locked to the barrel at the moment of firing. When fired, the explosion pressure inside the cartridge case drives it back and thus opens the breech. Safety is achieved by having the mass of the breech sufficient to resist the movement for the split second it takes the bullet to go up the barrel and leave the muzzle, after which the breech pressure drops; but by that time the breech has been given sufficient momentum for it to open.

Box Magazine

A form of ammunition supply where the cartridges are contained in a metal box, either detachable from the weapon or forming part of it, and are propelled towards the mouth of the magazine by a spring so as to enter the feedway of the weapon.

Calibre

The diameter of the weapon's barrel, measured internally from land to land, the land being that part of the barrel which lies between the rifling grooves. Alternatively, the diameter of a cylinder which will just pass through the barrel.

Caseless Cartridge

A cartridge which does not use the ordinary brass or other metal case to contain the propellant and carry the bullet and cap. It consists, instead, of a solid block of special propellant in which the bullet and cap are embedded; additionally, the cap is also of some combustible material. The result is that after firing there is no empty case or residue to be extracted, and thus reloading can take place much more quickly. It demands a very well sealed breech, since in an ordinary weapon the cartridge case expands to firm the seal.

Centre Fire

A cartridge in which the primer cap is placed centrally in the base.

Chamber

Enlarged and specially shaped portion of the barrel into which the cartridge is loaded in order to fire.

Cylinder

Component of a revolver in which the chambers are bored. This is held behind the barrel on an axis or arbor so that it can be revolved by some mechanism, usually connected to the trigger, so as to position each cylinder in turn behind the barrel.

Delayed Blowback

An automatic weapon in which the bolt is not positively locked to the barrel at the instant of firing but in which the rearward blowback movement of the bolt is slowed down by some mechanism so that there is resistance to opening until the bullet is well clear of the barrel.

Disconnector

Part of the firing mechanism of a self-loading weapon which disconnects the trigger after each shot and does not re-connect it until the firer releases the trigger. It prevents the weapon firing in automatic mode.

Double Action

A firing mechanism which permits two modes of operation. The hammer can be manually cocked and then released by pressing the trigger (single action); or the hammer can be cocked and released by a single continuous pressure on the trigger. Common in revolvers, less common in automatic pistols.

Gas Operation

A method of operating an automatic or self-cocking weapon. In the most common form, some of the gas driving the bullet is allowed to pass through a hole in the barrel and strike a piston-head; this is driven back and, in turn, forces back an operating arm which opens the breech and, at the same time, compresses a spring. The gas pressure is then allowed to escape and the spring expands, forcing the arm back to re-load and close the breech ready for the next shot.

Magazine Safety

A safety device in automatic pistols which prevents firing once the magazine has been removed. It prevents the common accident when a round is left in the chamber and later fired by someone who thought the gun was empty.

Receiver

The 'body' of a firearm, to which the barrel, stock, grip, sights and so on are attached, and inside which is the bolt or breech and firing mechanism.

Recoil Operation

Method of operation for a self-loading or automatic weapon which relies upon the recoil of the barrel after firing. May be 'long' or 'short' recoil; in the former, the barrel and closed breech move back a distance longer than the length of a complete cartridge, after which the breech is opened and held, while the barrel runs forward again. The breech is then released to load the weapon. In short recoil weapons the barrel and closed breech move back slightly, after which the breech is unlocked and the barrel stops, leaving the breech free to move back to complete the loading cycle.

Velocity

The speed of the bullet; generally given either in metres per second or feet per second. Defined as 'Muzzle Velocity' when referring to the speed as the bullet leaves the weapon; 'Observed Velocity', the speed at any particular point during its flight; and 'Remaining Velocity', the speed at the end of its flight.

Windage

Term used in two senses:- 1) the clearance between a muzzle-loaded bullet and the barrel, which allows the bullet to be loaded, or 2) an allowance given in taking aim so as to compensate for the effect of wind upon the bullet's flight. This can be done by moving the rear sight to one side or the other, and such movement is called 'windage'.

Zero

A weapon is 'zeroed' when the sights are adjusted so that the bullet will strike the point of aim at some specified distance. From this 'zero point' the sight adjustment mechanism will be able to alter the sight line for different ranges so that the bullet strike still coincides with the point of aim. But unless the zeroing is done by the person who intends to use the weapon, with the ammunition he intends to use, full benefit cannot be obtained, since the act of zeroing takes into account personal eyesight, the way he holds the weapon and other intangibles.